D1253658

SYNTAX AND STYLE
IN
OLD ENGLISH

SYNTAX AND STYLE
IN
OLD ENGLISH

by

S. O. ANDREW, M.A.

NEW YORK / RUSSELL & RUSSELL

1966

FIRST PUBLISHED IN 1940
REISSUED, 1966, BY RUSSELL & RUSSELL
A DIVISION OF ATHENEUM HOUSE, INC.
BY PERMISSION OF CAMBRIDGE UNIVERSITY PRESS
L.C. CATALOG CARD NO: 66—13220

PRINTED IN THE UNITED STATES OF AMERICA

CONTENTS

PREFACE

This short study is an attempt to drive a few main lines through the almost unexplored tract of Old English syntax. It began as an enquiry whether certain sentence-forms like Ða he answarode, Se wæs munuc on ðam mynstre, Hie ham on mergen foron, Ne ic cuðe him helpan (to cite a few out of many), which in all our printed OE texts, both prose and verse, appear frequently as principal sentences, can be accepted as such. The evidence seemed to the author conclusive that this question must be answered in the negative: the nature of the evidence and the method of investigation are briefly described in 34. As the enquiry proceeded, however, it began to appear that its scope must be enlarged, for each problem opened up new ones and in the end almost every type of principal and subordinate sentence had to be examined; in particular, the importance of defining clearly the different kinds of OE word-order, as a foundation for the enquiry as a whole, became apparent. Speaking generally, a study of prose and verse usage leads to the conclusion that the same rules hold for verse as for prose both in syntax and word-order; there are, however, some syntactical features peculiar to verse which demand separate consideration—the reader's attention may be drawn especially to the study of asyndetic co-ordination in Chapter VIII.

Perhaps the most important result of our investigation is the light which it throws on the characteristic features of OE style. The intimate connection of syntax and style is, of course, obvious, and almost every syntactical discussion in the book is indirectly also a discussion of style; Chapter XI deals directly with the problem of style and seeks to show that the supposed 'paratactic' structure of Old English, whether in prose or verse, is an illusion.

Reference is frequently made in the following pages to the 'traditional text' of *Beowulf*. By this is meant no more than the text as it is usually *punctuated* by editors; all the editions which I have consulted (Grein, Holthausen, Wyatt-Chambers, Sedgefield, Klaeber) agree, with only slight variations, in the punctuation of the poem and therefore in its syntactical interpretation so far as that is represented by punctuation.

S. O. A.

February, 1940.

TEXTS REFERRED TO, WITH
ABBREVIATIONS

PROSE (references are usually to page and line):

ASC	*Anglo-Saxon Chronicle*, ed. Plummer, Oxford.
Bede	*OE version of Bede's Eccl. History*, ed. Miller, EETS.
Blick.	*The Blickling Homilies*, ed. Morris, EETS.
CP	*Gregory's Cura Pastoralis*, ed. Sweet, EETS.
Gen., Exod., etc.	Books of Ælfric's OE Pentateuch in *Bibliothek der angelsächsischen Prosa*.
Hom.	*Ælfric's Homilies*, ed. Thorpe, Ælfric Society.
LS	*Ælfric's Lives of the Saints*, ed. Skeat, EETS.
Mat., Mk.	*OE Gospels*, ed. Skeat, Cambridge.
OET	*Oldest English Texts*, ed. Sweet, EETS.
Oros.	*Alfred's OE Translation of Orosius' History*, ed. Sweet, EETS.

VERSE (references are to line):

And.	Andreas	
Beo.	Beowulf	
Exod.	Exodus	in Grein-Wülker's *Bibliothek der*
Gen.	Genesis	*angelsächsischen Poesie*.
Jud.	Judith	
Mald.	Maldon	
Crist	Crist	
Guth.	Guthlac	in *Exeter Book I*, EETS.
Jul.	Juliana	
Wand.	Wanderer	
Best.	Bestiary	
Rid.	Riddles	
Soul's Ad.	Soul's Address	in *Exeter Book II*, EETS.
Wid.	Widsith	
Wulf	Wulf	

CHAPTER I

OLD ENGLISH WORD-ORDER

N.B. Numerals in heavier type, e.g. (38), refer to Sections.

1. Inspection of any OE prose text enables us to distinguish three different kinds of order in the OE sentence:

(i) *Common order* (subj. + verb + obj. + adverb), usual in principal sentences, e.g. Se cyning besæt hie on ðære ceastre, Manega leasa Cristas cumað on minum naman cweðende 'Ic eom Crist'. This is obviously the ancestor of our modern order; it may of course be varied in Old as in Modern English to give emphasis to a particular word, e.g. Tocwiesed hreod he ne forbriett 'A bruised reed he shall not break', but the inflectional character of OE allows an order no longer possible, e.g. Deman gedafenað setl, which we cannot render 'A judge befits sitting', since in modern English the order normally determines the syntax: Ælfric, however, uses either 'setl gedafenað deman' or 'deman gedafenað setl', according to the emphasis intended.

2. (ii) *Conjunctive order*, the normal one in subordinate clauses, e.g. þa he hie him eft ageaf 'when he had restored them to him', þær hie se cyning besæt 'where the King had besieged them'. Subordinate order might appear to be a good name for it, but, since it is found also after co-ordinating conjunctions, e.g. ond he gewundad wæs 'and he was wounded', ac he hine feor forwræc 'but he banished him far', and after many other conjunctives, e.g. relative pronouns and some adverbs when they stand first in the sentence, it will be more appropriate to speak of it as conjunctive order.

3. (iii) *Demonstrative order*, found in principal sentences after the demonstrative adverbs þa, þonne, þær, when they are head-words, e.g.:

Ða answarode he him. 'He then answered him.'
Ðonne cymð se Antecrist. 'Then shall come Anti-Christ.'
Ðær besæt hie se cyning. 'There the King besieged them.'

Sentences like 'ond þa he ferde to Rome', common in the *Anglo-Saxon Chronicle*, are no exception to the rule, since the head-word *ond* determines the order and *þa* is internal.

4. It will be well at this point to note the characteristic differences between demonstrative and conjunctive order. In the first, the verb has front position (after the head-word) with the pronouns immediately following; in the second, the pronouns stand all together immediately after the conjunctive, and quite separated, except accidentally, from the verb, which stands at the end. These differences appear clearly in almost any pair of correlated sentences, e.g.:

> Ðaða he slep, þa genom He an rib of his sidan.
> 'While he slept, God took a rib from his side.'
> Ðær he hine on þæm wuda gemette, þær ofslog he hine.
> 'He slew him just where he found him in the forest.'

It should be clearly understood that it is the position of the finite verb which matters; the end-position of the verbals in 'We sind of Criste cristene gehaten', 'he ne mihte þa gyt his Hælend gretan' is idiomatic, but it does not make the order in such sentences conjunctive. Contrariwise, in sentences like 'ond he ham eode to his huse', 'ær he acenned wæs of Marian', where an adverbial phrase stands after the verb as a sort of tag, the order is still conjunctive as the separation of the subject-pronoun from the finite verb shows.

5. Any page of prose will provide evidence that in Old as in Modern English the common order of the principal sentence is not infrequently retained in the subordinate clause, especially when the finite verb is an auxiliary, e.g. þa he wæs gewundad (instead of the normal 'þa he gewundad wæs'), and similarly in co-ordinate sentences after *ond*, *ac*, etc. Is this retention of common order permissible in the demonstrative sentence also? Can we (as in Modern English) say e.g. 'Ða he onswarode' instead of 'Ða onswarode he', or 'Ðær he besæt' instead of 'Ðær besæt he'? We shall attempt to answer this question in the two following chapters.

CHAPTER II

SENTENCES INTRODUCED BY ÐA

6. We begin with *þa*-sentences. In every OE prose text as printed principal sentences of the form 'þa he com' occur, and in some they abound. Are we to accept such sentences as representing good OE usage? The evidence of texts which are translations from Latin is here very instructive; wherever there is an obvious correlation, with or without correlating adverb, the supposed principal sentence turns out to be a subordinate clause. Here are four examples out of many from Ælfric's *Pentateuch*:

Gen. xxvii. 38.   Ða he swiðe weop. Ða wearð Isaac sarig
     xxxi. 21.   Þa he ferde mid þam þingum. Ða cyðde man Labane
Num. xii. 4.   Þa hi wæron ut agane; Drihten astah niðer on genipe
Deut. ix. 15.   Ða ic niðer eode of þam munte. Ic wearp þa bredu of minum handum

So Grein punctuates; the Latin, however, has Cumque fleret, Cumque abiisset, Cumque fuissent egressi, Cumque de monte ardente descenderem, for the four first sentences. It is important for our argument to remember that the punctuation of all our printed copies of OE texts is the work of modern editors; and the mere substitution of commas for other stops in each of the passages cited is enough to make the first sentence subordinate and the syntax normal. Instead of repeating this evidence for *Bede*, let us rather use that work to give examples of *þa*-sentences with common or conjunctive order which the Latin does certify as principal; they are six in number:

34. 26.   Þa S. Albanus gegyrede hine ða his munucgegyrelan
102. 20.   Þa se Godes wer is sægd þæt be forecwæde
252. 1.   [Þa þis þa gedon wæs] þa se biscop ond heora lareowas ham hwurfon
324. 21.   Þa Ðeodor þa ongunnon bernisse adwæscte
360. 12.   Þa þæt rice þa...fremde cyningas forluron
444. 8.   [Þa he þus gespræc] þa he...of worulde gewat

In all these, however, the readings on one ground or another are suspect: the first and fifth have a pleonastic *þa...þa* which is never found in principal sentences (some MSS. omit the first *þa* in 360. 12 and it ought to be omitted in 34. 26 also); the *þa* in 102. 20 translates Latin *quibus* (a continuative relative) and should be *þam* (=*þā*); the Latin in 252. 1 has 'et ipsi sacerdotes' ('the clerics also'), and one MS. actually has '*ond* se biscop'; in 324. 21, B, an excellent MS., omits the first *þa*, while in 444. 8 the same MS. instead of '*þa* he' has 'he *þa*', which as we shall see is normally followed by conjunctive order. The reader will be able to judge for himself how frail is the support for a '*þa* he com' form of principal sentence when he is assured that the six passages cited are the strongest evidence for it which can be produced. In the Gospels we have:

Matt. ix. 37. Ða he sæde. (*V*. Tum dicit.)
Mk. xiv. 10. Ða Iudas Scarioth, þæt is wiþersaca...ferde to þam heah-sacerdum. (*V*. Et Judas Iscariotes.)

Since translators usually followed the sacred text closely, 'Ða' is probably right in *Matt.* and 'ond' a certain correction in *Mark*; it may be noted, however, that the Lindisfarne version has 'ond' in both passages.

7. We turn now to OE texts which are not translations from Latin, and here our task will be to find an alternative interpretation of the sentence-form we are considering. To record and examine every supposed instance would obviously be a labour requiring a whole volume to itself; we shall therefore simplify the problem by excluding those instances (happily the great majority) in which correlation immediately suggests a different construction and only the editor's punctuation is at fault. Simple examples of such mis-punctuation are numerous in Ælfric's *Lives of the Saints*, both in text and translation, e.g.:

I. 32. Ða ic geseah þa halgan Godes gerynu. Ða wearp ic me sylfe forð on þa flor (where the translation has 'Then I beheld the holy mysteries. Then I cast myself, etc.').
II. 518. Ða he com ful neah into þære cypinge. Ða gehyrde he... (where the translation has 'And so he came into the market. Then he heard, etc.').

In each of these substitute a comma for the first full-stop. Other examples are not quite so simple; here are two from *ASC* 894:

(i) Ða he þa wæs þiderweardes ond sio oþeru fierd wæs hamweardes; ond ða Deniscan sæton þær behindan forþæm þe hiora cyning wæs gewundod on þæm gefeohte. Ða gegaderodon þa þe in Norþhymbrum bugeað sum hund scipa....

(ii) Ða se cyning hine þa west wende mid þære fierde wið Exancestres ond se here þa burg beseten hæfde; þa he þær to gefaren wæs, þa eodon hie to hiora scipum.

In both passages we have a single period with correlation. It may be said with confidence that the sentence-form 'þa he þa' (or, with a noun, 'þa se cyning þa') is in the *Chronicle*, as elsewhere, invariably subordinate; there are three examples in the paragraph immediately following the last passage cited. Moreover, the clause 'þa he þær to gefaren wæs' in (ii), catching up and amplifying the previous clause, is idiomatic in OE, e.g.:

Blick. 225*a*. Ða he þa hæfde þone hired gesibbodne ond þær dagas wel manige wæs, þa he þa eft mynte to his mynstre feran. Ða wearð he færinga swiðe untrum.

This should be read as a single period 'When he had made peace among the household and had now been among them many days, on his beginning to think of returning to his monastery he suddenly became very ill'; and similarly in *Bede* 36. 33:

Ða he þa mid swinglum wæced wæs ond he ealle þa witu geþyldelice abær. Ða se dema þæt þa oncneow...þa het he hine heafde beceorfan.

8. Excluding therefore sentences which, like those cited, obviously admit of another and very idiomatic construction, let us now examine those passages in the chief OE prose-writers which seem at first sight to present veritable instances of the 'þa he com' type in principal sentences. We begin with the *Homilies* of Ælfric, in which by general consent are to be found the finest examples of the mature OE prose style:

Hom. I. 26. 29. He nolde geniman us neadunge of deofles anwealde buton he hit forwyrhte; þa he hit forwyrhte genoh swiðe þaða he gehwette and tihte ðæra Iudeiscra manna heortan to Cristes slege.

So Thorpe, making two principal sentences. We have better sense, and the sense we expect, if we take the second sentence as a causal clause qualifying the previous sentence, 'He would not have taken us by force from the devil's power unless the devil had forfeited his power, since he did indeed forfeit it altogether when he whetted the hearts of the Jews to the slaying of Christ'.

Hom. I. 144. 14. Þa Maria, þæt halige mæden, and þæs cildes fostor-fæder wæron ofwundrode þæra worda....And se Symeon him ða sealde bletsunge.

If the text is good, this must be admitted as a veritable instance of the 'ða he com' form; though it may be pointed out that the mere omission of 'And' would give us a period in which the second sentence is principal and the first subordinate. This construction would be possible in *Bede* or *Blickling* even with the 'And', since we frequently find *and* in apodosis in these texts; it does not occur however in Ælfric.

Hom. I. 152. 24. Þa eal þæt folc, þe þæt wundor geseh, herede God....

This is the end of a long quotation from St Luke's Gospel (xviii. 43); the reading in the Gospel text is 'ond (not þa) eal þæt folc', and we can hardly doubt that 'þa' is a scribal error: the *ond*-sigil (7) was frequently confused by copyists with þa. The Vulgate has 'Et omnis plebs...'.

Hom. I. 418. 21. Ða se eadiga Laurentius ðwoh heora ealra fet and ða wudewan from hefigtimum heafod-ece gehælde. Eac sum ymesene man mid wope his fet gesohte biddende his hæle.

Thorpe's punctuation misses the point of the sentence before, which tells us how L. distributed alms to poor strangers and widows, and at last came to a widow called Quiriaca who had given shelter to many persecuted persons, and (he continues) '*when* the blessed man had washed the feet of them all and relieved the widow of a troublesome head-ache, a blind man also sought his feet, weeping and praying for a cure'. The syntax is quite normal.

Hom. I. 482, ft. Þa, forðam ðe he nolde from his gebeorum beon gecweden manswara, ðone beorscipe mid blode gemencgde. 'Then, because he would not be called a perjurer, [he] stained the banquet with blood.'

The subjectless 'gemencgde' is a certain sign that the sentence is co-ordinate to 'Herodes swor þæt he wolde hire forgyfan swa hwæt swa heo bæde' just before and has the same subject: *ond* has therefore been omitted before '*þa*' and the adverb is no longer the head-word.

Hom. II. 6. 12. Þa æfre smeade God fram frymðe middaneardes hu he mihte mancynnes gehelpan.... Þa nolde he asendan to ure alysednysse naðor ne engel ne heah-engel... ac sende se Fæder his ancennedan sunu.

Thorpe translates 'Then God ever meditated how he might help mankind. Then he would not send, etc.' There is, however, a far more natural meaning, viz. '*Since* God was always thinking from the beginning of the world how he might help mankind, he would not send for our redemption either angel or archangel, but sent his only-begotten Son.' The syntax is normal and the sense what the argument requires.

Hom. II. 212. 21. Ða Iordanis seo ea on emtwa toeode.

Thorpe renders 'Then the Jordan separated into two parts'. Ælfric is describing the stages by which Israel reached the promised land: after the death of Moses they begat a great progeny in the wilderness, they then came under Joshua to the nations to which they had been called 'when the river Jordan parted in two and they went over dryshod'; here we have the continuative *ða* (38) common in Ælfric.

Hom. II. 260. 28. Ða sum rice ðegen ðearle wæs gelyfed on Dryhten, his nama wæs Joseph: and he genealæhte ða hrædlice to ðam ealdormen.

This passage is exactly like *Hom.* I. 144. 14 just above and the same explanation applies. There is no need to cite instances in which a sentence is introduced by *Hwæt þa* or *Efne þa*, since the usage both of Ælfric and other writers makes it quite clear that interjections like *Hwæt* and *Efne* were normally followed by conjunctive order, e.g.:

Hom. I. 78. 28. Hwæt þa God on swefne hi gewarnode. 'Lo! then God warned them in a dream.'

The *þa* in such phrases was no doubt enclitic to the interjection and unstressed.

9. Our examination of the *Homilies* has left us with possibly two examples of the '*þa* he com' type of principal sentence. If we may take the Homilies on St Cuthbert or St Benedict as a standard,

there are on the average four and a half demonstrative þa-sentences to a page, and, therefore, some 2700 in the work as a whole. This gives us less than one exception to every thousand examples of the normal construction, a proportion which can easily be accounted for by scribal error. Let us now pass to *Orosius* (included here because the Latin original throws no light on the passages cited):

Oros. 46. 7. Þa under þæm gewinne hie genamon frið wið þa wæpnedmenn. Siþþan wæs hiera þeaw....

Read as one sentence and we have good sense and normal syntax: 'When they had made peace with the men, it was ever after their custom, etc.'

Oros. 62. 7. And þa þæt eastrice in Asiria gefeoll, þa þæt westrice in Roma aras.

This sentence is the second member of a clause following 'Swa gelomp þætte' and should be so punctuated: 'so it befell that [just when Babylon became subject to Cyrus Rome was delivered from the Tarquins] and just when the Eastern Empire fell in Assyria the Western Empire arose in Rome.' The syntax is normal, the conjunctive order of 'þa...aras' being determined by 'ond [þætte]' which (and not þa) is the head-word. Examples might be multiplied; here is one:

Bede 400. 27. Ða ic hreowsende wæs, ða ic mid ðy heafde com on þone stan dryfan.

Here also the sentence depends on 'Ða gelomp' and should be so pointed; it may be observed that in this passage two MSS. read 'þæt' for the second 'þa', which makes the interpretation given quite certain.

Oros. 284. 33. Þa he þæt geascade, þa he gefor on þam færelte. 'Having learnt this, he died on his journey.'

This looks like a certain instance, but fortunately the C manuscript, a better authority, reads 'þa gefor he' and enables us to correct it.

The *Chronicle* abounds in þa-sentences, and here if anywhere we might expect to find indubitable instances of the 'þa he com' type of principal sentence if they exist at all. Yet the only one of the kind is:

ASC 762 (E). Þa man gehalgode Pyhtwine to bisceop. 'Then P. was consecrated bishop.'

Even for this exceptional instance a simple explanation is possible; in the early annals of the *Chronicle* the more usual connective is not þa but 'ond þa', as in 755 just before where it occurs eight times, and 'ond þa' in our passage would make the syntax normal, *ond* and not þa being the head-word. One remarkable feature of the evidence from the *Chronicle* ought to be mentioned: we frequently find in its pages six or eight þa-sentences in succession, and if the 'þa he com' type had been a real one there could hardly have failed to be instances of *two* such sentences in sequence, which no repunctuation could have made into a correlated pair. It can scarcely be luck that whenever we find a supposed instance of the 'þa he com' type there is, except in the passage just cited, the appropriate demonstrative sentence next to it.

10. This concludes our survey of the evidence for the 'þa he com' form of principal sentence in the five principal works of OE prose. We have found that almost all the supposed instances of it are explicable by the rules of normal syntax and that even the half-dozen exceptions are, for one reason or another, not of a kind to carry conviction; we are justified therefore in concluding that in prose this sentence-form is unambiguously subordinate.

11. Let us now go on to consider the further problem whether the 'þa com he' type, which is usually a principal sentence, is unambiguously so or may also be a subordinate clause. It will be necessary to examine the evidence carefully since the wide prevalence of the clause seems not to be generally realized; no example of it is given by Sweet in his excellent *Primer* among the sentences which form Chapter I, although these illustrate almost every other type of OE clause; and the editors of texts almost invariably print such clauses as principal sentences, especially when the verb is stressed, e.g.:

Matt. viii. 18. Ða geseah se Hælend þa menigu; þa het he hig faran.

The Vulgate has 'videns autem Iesus...', and there is, therefore, a strong presumption that the first sentence is a temporal clause— 'when Jesus saw the multitude'. Let us apply the same test to a few other passages (which might be greatly multiplied) from works which are translations from the Latin:

Gen. xxxii. 25. Þa geseah he þæt he hine oferswiðan ne mihte; þa æthran he....

Exod. ii. 12. Þa beseah he hine ymbutan...; þa ofsloh he þone Egyptiscan.

So Grein points, making two pairs of demonstrative sentences. The Vulgate, however, has 'Cum videret quod eum superare non posset, tetigit, etc.', and 'Cum circumspexisset, percussum Aegyptium [abscondit]', and there can be little doubt that the first sentence in each of the OE passages should be taken as a temporal clause.

Oros. 156. 29. Ða ascedan hiene his þegnas....Ða ondwyrde he.

234. 21. Ða bæd he þæt mon þone triumphan him ongean brohte. Ða sende mon....

So Sweet, making two pairs of demonstrative sentences. But in each passage the Latin begins with a temporal clause 'cum a sociis increparetur' and 'cum nuncios de victoria misisset', and again there can be little doubt that we should render 'when his thanes asked him' and 'when he demanded a triumph'.

Bede 118. 6. Þa for se wallende leg..., þa getreowde he in godcundne fultum.

166. 28. Þa com he ærest on Westseaxum, þa þuhte him....

So Miller correctly, as the Latin shows, 'cum furens se flamma dilataret', etc.

12. Such passages establish quite clearly the 'þa com he' type of subordinate clause as a genuine OE idiom. It would be wearisome to review further examples at length, but it may be worth while to indicate briefly and in general terms the kind of context in which a clause is specially appropriate. Wherever a sentence like 'þa gehyrde he', 'þa befran he hine', is followed immediately by another of the same form, e.g. þa cwæð he, the juxtaposition usually demands correlation; here are three examples:

Hom. II. 310. 1. Ða befran se arleasa casere hwi he suwode. Ða
sæde se halga wer....

Oldest ET 178. 36. Ða frægn se þegn for hwon he suæ dide; þa
cwæð he....

LS 200. 165. Ða geseah þæs scypes hlaford þæt heo fæger wæs; þa
gewilnade he hi habban.

One sentence: 'When the shipmaster saw that she was fair, he
desired to possess her.'

Our rule applies especially to examples from the mature prose of
Ælfric and his school, in which a sequence of emphatic *þa*-sentences,
appropriate enough in the early *Chronicle* or in the speech of the
simple seaman Ohthere, is generally speaking studiously avoided;
e.g. in

Hom. II. 150. 22. Ða gesæt he æt mysan, micclum onbryrd he beseah
to heofonum ond his sex awearp. Ða axode hine seo eadige fæmne hwi
he his gereord forlete? Ða cwæð se bisceop....

the last two sentences should be punctuated as one: 'When the
blessed woman asked him why he left his meal, the bishop
answered....'

13. It will now be clear that the sentence-form 'þa com he' is in
prose ambiguous, and can be either principal or subordinate. This
being so, it may be pointed out that if a *þa*-sentence with common
or conjunctive order is also, as many apparently believe, ambiguous, i.e. may be either principal or subordinate, then all the
þa-sentence forms were interchangeable; that is to say, *each* of the
sentences Þa he wæs gewundad, Þa he gewundad wæs, Þa wæs he
gewundad, could mean either '*when* he was wounded' or '*then* he
was wounded'. Can we credit such a complete confusion of types?

14. We shall now consider the two sentence-forms in poetry. It
will be convenient to begin with the 'þa com he' form and we shall
confine ourselves for the present to examples in which the verb is a
stress-word. When we search for such examples, we make the
astonishing discovery that the 'þa com he' type, perhaps the most
common in OE prose, is in verse hardly to be found at all. Leaving
out of account for the moment the question whether they are
principal or subordinate, there are only five such sentences in
Beowulf (all 'þa com'), seven in *Andreas* (five of them by a curious

chance 'þa com'), three in *Juliana* (again all 'þa com'), one in *Maldon* ('þa stod', l. 25), and none in *Judith* or *Crist*. We shall confine our attention for the present to the instances from *Beowulf*, which are:

710	Ða com of more,...Godes yrre bær
1162	Gamen eft astah,
	beorhtmode bencsweg. Ða com Wealhþeo forð
1600	Ða com non dæges; næs ofgeafon
1644	Ða com inn [gan]gan ealdor ðegna.
	Ða wæs be feaxe on flet boren
	Grendles heafod
1802	Ða com beorht scacan
	[Scima æfter sceadwe]; scaþan onetton.

Are these sentences principal or subordinate? The traditional text (see any of the modern editions) punctuates the last four (as shown) as principal sentences, and probably the first is also intended in the same way; to this there is the fatal metrical objection that in all except the first we have then *four* stresses to the half-line (þá cóm nón dǽges) except on the quite unproven assumption that the adverb *þa* could in verse be stressed or unstressed at pleasure.[1] There is no metrical objection to taking *þa* as a conjunction (unstressed), the first example being then Sievers' A type with anacrusis, and the other four his D or E types, also with anacrusis; and the sense is good:

'When he came from the moor, God's wrath he bare.'
'There was revel once more and clamour on bench, when W. came forth.'
'When came the ninth hour, they left the ness.'
'When the chief had entered, then was the head of Grendel borne into hall.'
'When came the bright sunlight, warriors hastened.'

It seems, therefore, that all these sentences must be taken as subordinate clauses. The absence from *Beowulf* (and from poetry generally) of such a common type as the demonstrative sentence is certainly surprising, but the existence of the five given, if they were all conceded as principal sentences, would be no less surprising;

---

[1] Sievers, for example, makes the first an A type, stressing *þa* and unstressing *com*; the rest he makes C types, unstressing both *þa* and *com*.

there are often five instances on a single page of prose, and five in over 3000 lines would represent a degree of rarity as conspicuous as total absence, and would need a good deal of explaining. There is indeed cogent evidence that poetic convention deliberately eschewed the 'þa com' form in principal sentences; for in verses like

620   Ymbeode þa ides Helminga
1870   Gecyste þa cyning æþelum god

we never find in *Beowulf* the order 'þa ymbeode' or 'þa gecyste' (though it is just as good both metrically and in syntax) except where *þa* is not the head-word as in 630 'ond þa gyddode'. In *Andreas*, it must be admitted, we have instances, 'þa reordade' 415, 'þa hleoþrade' 537, but usually this type is confined to unstressed verbs, with which, of course, it is quite common, e.g.:

Beo. 128   Þa wæs æfter wiste wop up ahafen.
138   Þa wæs eaðfynde þe him elles hwær....

15. What then, it may be asked, are the sentence-forms with a stressed verb which in poetry take the place of the demonstrative type which is the rule in prose? They are two in number, the 'com þa' form and the 'he þa' form:

(i) The 'com þa' form marks a rapid transition from speech to action or from one action to another. When there is no change of subject, the subject-pronoun is not expressed (as frequently in prose also, e.g. Foron þa upp, Eodon þa inn, in the *Chronicle*); *Beo.* 1563, He gefeng þa fetelhilt, if really an instance, is unique. There are in *Beowulf* about 90 instances of the 'com þa' form, and we are justified in asking those who make 'þa com' a principal sentence what is the difference between 'þa com' and 'com þa', and why the poet uses the first in

710   Ða com of more...Grendel gongan

and the second just below,

720   Com þa of recede rinc siðian

If our argument has been correct, there is a difference of grammar, the first example being a temporal clause.

(ii) When for any reason the poet wishes to express the pronoun-subject he uses the form 'he þa', e.g.:

2135   Ic þa ðæs wælmes grundhyrde fond.
        'Then did I seek out the warder of the abyss.'
2788   He þa mid maðmum mærne þioden [fand].
        'Then did he find, when he brought the gifts, the
            mighty prince [at life's end].'

If the subject is a noun, a *governed* pronoun may stand before the 'þa', e.g.:

Beo. 3137   Him þa gegiredon Geata leode.
        'Then did the Geat-folk make ready for him....'
Jud. 94   Hi þa se hehsta Dema
        ædre mid elne onbryrde.
        'Her then did the Highest straightway inspire with
            courage.'

The 'he þa' form is particularly common in *Judith*. It will be observed from the examples given that conjunctive order is generally, though not exclusively, found after this phrase.

It may be surmised that in the 'com þa' form the adverb was enclitic to the verb, and in the 'he þa' form the pronoun was proclitic to the adverb; however this may have been, the latter form certainly enabled the poet to solve a metrical difficulty in many half-lines like 'hi þa hine hwetton', where the normal prose order 'þa hwetton hi hine' would have presented a falling rhythm ending in four unstressed syllables.

16. Let us now turn to the 'þa he com' form in poetry. For reasons of space we shall confine our survey to *Beowulf* and to those þa-sentences in the poem which all the modern editions agree in punctuating as principal sentences. We begin with five instances of conjunctive order:

461   ða hine Wedera cyn
        for herebrogan habban ne mihte.
        [Ðanon he gesohte Suð-dena folc]
518   þa hine on morgentid
        on Heaðo-Ræmas holm up ætbær;
        [ðonon he gesohte swæsne eðel]
579   [siþes werig.] Ða mec sæ oþbær

662   Ða him Hroðgar gewat...ut of healle;
               [Hæfde Kyning-wuldor
           seleweard aseted]
671   Ða he him of dyde isern-byrnan...
           [Gespræc þa se goda].

The conjunctive order in these sentences (position of pronouns,
and the inversion 'of dyde') marks them as unmistakably subordinate unless it can be shown that poetic usage differed from that
of prose; the sentences or phrases which they qualify are given in
brackets. The only type of *principal* sentence in which conjunctive
order is idiomatic is (as we have seen) the 'he þa' form; and 'he þa
him of dyde', 'Him þa Hroðgar gewat' (cf. 26 Him þa Scyld gewat),
etc., would be good grammar and good metre, if the poet had
chosen to use them. Those who take the sentences as principal
must also be prepared to defend the three-lift metrical type in a
b-verse (þá mec sǽ oþbǽr) unless they can prove that the adverb
þa could be unstressed. If the sentences are taken as subordinate,
the sense is good and the syntax normal.

17. There is another group which may be considered together, of
which the following are examples:

229   Þa of wealle geseah weard Scyldinga...
                    [hine fyrwyt bræc]
809   Ða þæt onfunde se þe fela æror
           fyrene gefremede...
           þæt him se lichoma læstan nolde...
                    [wæs gehwæþer oþrum
           lifigende lað]

These are simply varieties of the 'þa com he' type of subordinate
clause already discussed, with an adverb or object preceding the
verb. The second passage is interesting; there does not seem to be
any certified instance in prose of a *double* demonstrative (e.g. 'þa
þæt', 'þa þær') beginning a principal sentence, and in poetry also
such a double stress was evidently avoided. If that is the case, the
þa in such collocations is always the conjunction, as in

1598   þa þæs monige gewearð
           þæt hine seo brimwylf abroten hæfde
           'since it seemed to many that the seawolf had destroyed
              him'.

which most editors punctuate as a subordinate clause. Similarly in

331   [wæs se irenþreat
wæpnum gewurðad.] Ða þær wlonc hæleð
oretmecgas æfter æþelum frægn

the 'þa þær' sentence should be taken as a temporal clause: 'that
mailèd band was worthily weaponed when a proud warrior asked
them there of their lineage.'

18. In the next group (see also 112) we have examples of
correlation:

1512   Ða se eorl ongeat
þæt he in niðsele nathwylcum wæs...
[Ongeat þa se goda grundwyrgenne]

2131   Þa se ðeoden mec ðine life
healsode hreohmod...
[Ic þa ðæs wælmes, þe is wide cuð,
                     ...grundhyrde fond]

2715   Ða se æðeling giong...
[Hyne þa mid handa...wætere gelafede].

In the first passage 'Ongeat' (in 1514) is strange after the first
'ongeat' and is perhaps a mere echo of it. In

1605   þa þæt sweord ongan,
wigbil wanian; [þæt wæs wundra sum...]

2312   Ða se gæst ongan gledum spiwan
                        [bryneleoma stod
eldum on andan.]

2711   Ða sio wund ongon
swelan ond swellan; [he þæt sona onfand
þæt him on breostum bealoniðe weoll]

the clause is followed by an ordinary principal sentence, without
correlative adverb. There are three passages in which a subordinate
construction of the þa-clause is important for the meaning:

86   Ða se ellorgæst earfoðlice
þrage geþolode, se þe in þystrum bad,
þæt he dogora gehwam dream gehyrde.

This is usually taken to mark the introduction of Grendel, who,

however, is not mentioned till l. 102. Does it not refer to the
jealousy of the Prince of Darkness which caused the troubles of
the Royal House described in the lines just before—the burning of
Hart and the murderous feud of King and son-in-law? The visita-
tion of Grendel was, of course, a consequence of this jealousy. The
sense would be 'loathly flame it (Hart) awaited, nor was it long
e'en then ere the murderous strife awoke of marriage-kin, *since* the
Alien Spirit that dwelt in darkness could not endure the joy in
hall...'. This makes explicit the motive, otherwise only to be
guessed, for the attacks on Hart.

1095   Ða hie getruwedon on twa healfa
                        fæste frioðu-wære; Fin Hengeste
                        elne unflitme aðum benemde...

Does not the clause mark the transition from the first stage of the
action to the second in which Finn is brought, for the first time,
on to the stage? 'When they (his thanes) had plighted a trusty
peace, Finn confirmed it by solemn oaths....' This interpretation
accords with the view, which clears up many difficulties in the
story, that Finn was not responsible for the treacherous attack on
the Half-Danes but only came on the scene later to compose a
tribal feud.

1698   Ða se wisa spræc
              sunu Healfdenes—swigedon ealle—

In any case, it may be observed, there is no reason for taking the
first sentence as principal and making the second a parenthesis;
the natural meaning is 'When the wise one spake, they were silent
all'. The clause, however, is in this context specially appropriate,
since it catches up 'Hrodgar maðelode', ten lines before, after the
long interruption; to render it *'then* he *spoke'* would be mere
tautology. There remain only the five 'þa ic gefrægn' instances,
which, however, must wait for another chapter. The instances we
have dealt with have, it may be hoped, been sufficient to convince
the reader that a simple repunctuation, without any emendation of
the text, provides an alternative construction for all of them, i.e.
the construction which everyone admits is the normal one for that
type of sentence. It must be added that many of the ambiguous

'*þa* wæs' sentence-forms (almost invariably pointed as principal in the traditional text) are better taken as subordinate, e.g.:

917   Ða wæs morgenleoht
                   scofen ond scynded. Eode scealc monig...

3033   Fundon ða on sande sawulleasne
                   hlimbed healdan...; *þa* wæs endedæg
                   godum gegongen

Other examples are 126, 467, 1008, 1136, 1399, 2580.

19. Our conclusions in this chapter may be summarised as follows:

(i) sentences of the form '*þa* he com' are, both in prose and verse, always subordinate clauses, and are, therefore, unambiguous;

(ii) sentences of the form '*þa* wæs he', though usually principal sentences, may both in prose and verse be also subordinate clauses, and are, therefore, ambiguous;

(iii) in prose, sentences of the form '*þa* com he' (i.e. in which the verb is stressed), though usually principal sentences, may be subordinate clauses, and are, therefore, ambiguous;

(iv) sentences of the form '*þa* com he' are in *Beowulf*, and most other OE poetry, unambiguously subordinate clauses.

It is perhaps not unnecessary to add that the ambiguity spoken of is only true of the sentence-forms as they are written; in speech, principal sentences must always have been differentiated from clauses, *þa* (adv.) being stressed and *þa* (conj.) unstressed.

CHAPTER III

ÐÆR- AND ÐONNE-SENTENCES

20. We shall follow the same method in this chapter as in the last, and begin with all the supposed instances from *Bede* and *Orosius* of principal sentences with common or conjunctive order in which *þær* is the head-word; the Latin text is given beside them:

Bede 92. 18. wæs gefeoht on þære stowe þe cweden is Degsastan. Ðær lytestne eal his weorud ofslegen wæs (in loco qui dicitur D. omnis pene eius est caesus exercitus)

212. 2. Ðær he wæs mid untrymnesse þread (ubi correptus infirmitate, etc.)

256. 23. Ðær hine gestod sumu untrymnis (ubi fatigatus infirmitate, etc.)

262. 12. Ðær gen to dæge seðel is þara biscopa (ubi usque hodie sedes est).

292. 25. Ðær heo wæs ondettende (ubi fidem professa est)

358. 16. Ðær eac swylce se arwurða Trumwine gewat (ubi Trumwine recessit)

Oros. 8. 26. Ðær eac Ercoles syla standað (ubi H. columnae visuntur)

14. 10. Ðær of þæm beorgum wilþ seo ea suþweard (qui de radice montis effusus etc.)

138. 12. Ðær on þam gefeohte wæs Cuintus ofslagen (in quo bello etc.)

176. 16. Ðær heora wæron ix M ofslagen (proelioque commisso novem M perdiderunt).

In no instance, it will be observed, does *þær* render the Latin demonstrative adverb; in all but two, the first and last, where the Latin and English are turned differently, the Latin positively indicates a subordinate clause, and this is the natural construction in the two others.

21. Let us now examine supposed exceptions in texts not translated from Latin. We can simplify our problem as before by excluding many instances for which there is an obvious alternative explanation: first, correlated sentences like 'þær he hine gemette:

þær ofslog he hine', where repunctuation makes the first sentence a normal subordinate clause; and, secondly, sentences like 'ond þær eac seo cwen bebyrged is', where the head-word is not *þær* but *ond*, after which conjunctive order is the rule. In Ælfric's *Hom.* I. 386. 13 we have 'Far forð to ðære byrig: þær þe bið gesæd hwæt ðe gedafenige'. This is a quotation from *Acts* ix. 6, where the Vulgate has 'et ibi dicetur tibi', and there can be no doubt that *ond* has been omitted before *þær*; in fact *Hom.* I. 124. 22, where the same quotation occurs, has 'ond þær ðe bið gesæd'. In *Matt.* xviii. 20 we have 'þær twegen oððe þry sind gegaderode þær ic eom on hyra midlene', but the Vulgate has 'ubi *enim* sunt duo vel tres, etc.', and again there can be little doubt that in the English a con-junction has been omitted which would make the order normal. A curious exception to the rule is *Hom.* II. 442. 31 þæt þæt Martha dyde þær we sind, whatever be the sense of it. In *CP* 115. 21 He cwæð þæt he wære his gelica: ðær he gecyðde his eaðmodnesse, remove the colon; *þær* introduces a clause with the idiomatic meaning 'whereby he showed his humility'. And so in *Hom.* II. 556. 21: Ðær he þolað neadunge þeostra ðurh wrace seðe ær forbær his unlustes þeostra; attach the sentence to the previous one and we have the sense we expect '(the outer blindness) whereby, as retribution, he suffers darkness who had before endured the dark-ness of evil desire'. Again, in *ASC* 565 Ðær se Columba getym-brade mynster, we have an obvious antecedent to *þær* in 'þæt eglond þe man nemnad Ii' just before. But in *ASC* 607 þær man sloh eac cc preosta, the explanation may lie in the omission of *ond*, since 'ond þær' 'ond þa' are the usual connectives in the early parts of the *Chronicle*.

22. We pass to *þonne*-sentences, and begin by reminding the reader of the difference in usage between *þonne* and *þa*. Whether as adverb or conjunction, *þonne* (not *þa*) is regularly used in present or future temporal sentences; in past temporal sentences both words are used but with a distinction of meaning, *þonne* being invariably frequentative whereas *þa* is restricted to a particular occasion, e.g. *Bede* 342. 22, þonne he geseah þa hearpan him nealæcan þonne aras he for scome from þæm symble. Þa he þæt þa sumre tide dyde..., 'Whenever he saw the harp approach him he

always withdrew for very shame from the feast. And when he did so on one occasion, etc.' Instances like

> *Bede* 152. 9. Ðonne feng to Beornica rice Æþelfriðes sunu
> 280. 12. Ðonne wæs Biise Eastengla biscop,

where *þonne* seems to be used instead of *þa*, are only apparent exceptions, for *þonne* is here not a temporal adverb but renders the Latin *porro* or *autem*. Order, as well as meaning, disallows a temporal sense in 442. 21 Ðonne him gelomp...; here the Latin has *unde*, and *þonne* must be a scribal error for *þonon* ('hence it happened', cf. 178. 5); in 84. 17 þonne se wer seþe wætre aþwegen bið mot þæm geryne onfon, the Latin has again *autem*. There is in fact no instance in *Bede* or *Orosius* of *þonne* (=then) being followed in a principal sentence by anything but demonstrative order.

23. Let us now turn to the supposed exceptions in non-Latin texts. Here also we simplify our problem by excluding sentences in which *þonne* (adv.) is not the head-word: e.g. *Blick.* 93 mid., ond þonne hit bið æt sumum setlgange, *Hom.* I. 612. 17 forðam ðonne hi gemetað þone ðe hi lufodon; and those also in which correlation points to an alternative construction, e.g. *Hom.* I. 172. 20 Ðonne bið he deofles þeowa; þonne he deofle gecwemð. I. 460 ft., Ðonne geswicð he þære gedreccednysse: þonne hi cweðað 'Ðu eart min God'. Thorpe translates each of these as two principal sentences ('then is he the devil's thrall, then is he acceptable to the devil') completely spoiling the sense; we have normal syntax and the sense we expect if we take the second sentence in each as subordinate. *Hom.* II. 364. 4 þonne bið us Godes oncwawennys fulfremed, þonne þær nan deað ne bið, þonne we God geseoð is not quite so simple; Thorpe translates 'then will our knowledge of God be perfect, then will there be no death, then shall we see God'; the last two sentences, however, are subordinate and mean 'since there will be no death when we see God'. *Hom.* II. 378. 2 Ðonne hi clypiað to me and ic hi ne gehyre; looks like a real exception, but the version of this OT text in *CP* 248. 3 is Ðonne hi to me clipiað, þonne nyle ic hie gehieran: omit 'and' in the *Hom.* passage. We have an interesting example of a different kind in *CP* 161. 12: Ðonne hie lecgeað þa tieglan beforan hie, þonne hi behealdað ða inngeþoncas hiora modes. The reading 'ond þonne hie lecgeað'

would make *þonne* internal and the syntax normal: the writer is interpreting the text Genim *þe* ane tigelan *ond* lege beforan *þe* 'take thee a tile and lay it before thee', and we expect the allegorical application to be similarly bimembral. He has already dealt with the first clause 'The holy teachers take a tile when, etc.' and we look for a second '*and* they lay the tile before them when they look at their innermost thoughts'. That this is the natural form of sentence might be proved by many examples: in 172. 4 the author is interpreting the command 'to put the staves in the ark and lift it up stoutly', and after expounding the first clause he continues Ond *þonne* hie hæbbað arudlice *þa* earce up *þonne* hie bioð gearwe to læranne 'and they then lift the ark up stoutly when they are ready to teach'. It is perhaps hardly likely that the second of such a pair of sentences should be asyndetical and still retain the word-order usual after the conjunction: but if it is possible, the passage we are commenting on would be regular even without the restoration of *ond*.

24. All the evidence then points to the conclusion that sentences of the form '*þær* (*þonne*) he stod' are unambiguously subordinate. Let us pause here for a moment and consider the complementary problem whether sentences of the form '*þær* (*þonne*) stod se cyning', which are admittedly principal sentences as a rule, are unambiguously so. The evidence of translated texts is clear:

Bede 324. 9. *þær* wilnode mynster habban seo gemyndgode Cristes *þeowe* (ubi monasterium habere desideravit etc.).

Oros. 104. 7. *þær* gefeaht Manlius anwig (ubi pugnam M. singulariter inchoavit).

160. 4. *þær* onfundan Cartaginenses *þæt* hi mon oferswiðan mehte (ubi C. vinci se posse senserunt), i.e. 'whereby the C. discovered that they could suffer defeat'.

and so even where the verb is *is* or *wæs*, e.g.

Oros. 28. 6. *þær* is seo burh neah *þe* mon hæt Libeum (ubi et civitas ejusdem nominis est).

All these are printed as principal sentences in the EETS. texts. There does not appear to be any instance with *þonne* in a translated work, but in contexts like *Hom.* II. 52. 9 Ðonne axað he gyt 'Gelyfst ðu?' He andwyrt 'ic gelyfe', the first sentence may well mean 'When he again asks'. We conclude therefore that sentences of the form 'þær (þonne) stod he' are, at least in prose, ambiguous, i.e. may be either principal or subordinate.

25. Let us now test both our rules in poetry, confining ourselves, from considerations of space, chiefly to *Beowulf*. There are about forty places in the poem in which one edition or another punctuates a sentence of the form 'þær he geseah' as a principal sentence; we shall deal here with those instances only which all the modern editions are agreed in so punctuating. Let us first, however, draw attention to a difference in the treatment of similar sentences which is very puzzling; here is a pair with exactly the same kind of conjunctive order:

$\begin{cases} 1269 \\ 866 \end{cases}$ Đær him aglæca ætgræpe wearð
ðær him foldwegas fægere þuhton

yet all the editors punctuate the first as a principal and the second as a subordinate sentence. And so in the pairs

$\begin{cases} 1190 \\ 1163 \end{cases}$ þær se goda sæt
þær þa godan twegen...sæton

$\begin{cases} 1470 \\ 2787 \end{cases}$ þær he dome forleas
þær he hine ær forlet

On what principle do they discriminate between them? In all six alike a subordinate clause yields the best sense, and the order makes such a clause certain.

26. We can now consider the principal sentences (so printed in all our texts) in which *þær* is followed by an order other than demonstrative. Unless the usage of poetry can be proved to be different from that of prose, these must all be subordinate clauses; and this construction gives excellent sense:

440   [ac ic mid grape sceal
         fon wið feonde;]...   ðær gelyfan sceal
         Dryhtnes dome   se þe hine deað nimeð

513   þær git eagorstream earmum þehton;
         [geofon yðum weol]

977   [balwon bendum;]   ðær abidan sceal
         maga mane fah   miclan domes

1190   þær se goda sæt.
         [Him wæs ful boren]

1269   [se æt Heorote fand
        wæccendne wer wiges bidan.]
        Ðær him aglæca   ætgræpe wearð
1365   [wudu wyrtum fæst   wæter oferhelmað.]
        Ðær [man] mæg nihta gehwæm   niðwundor seon
1470   [selfa ne dorste
        drihtscype dreogan;]   þær he dome forleas
2137   [Ic þa ðæs wælmes...   grundhyrde fond.]
        Ðær unc hwile wæs   handgemæne

In all these we have conjunctive (note the inversions 'gelyfan
sceal', etc.) or common order; in the following we have the special
order seen in 'ða of wealle geseah', already discussed (17):

32   [...to brimes faroðe.]
        Ðær æt hyðe stod   hringedstefna
775   [þæt he on hrusan ne feol,
        fæger foldbold...]   Ðær fram sylle abeag
        medubenc monig
794   [ne his lifdagas   leoda ænigum
        nytte tealde.]   Ðær genehost brægd
        eorl Beowulfes   ealde lafe
1243   [Setton him to heafdon   hilderandas...]
                         þær on bence wæs
        ofer æþelinge   yðgesene
        heaþosteapa helm
2214   [stanbeorh steapne   stig under læg]
                         Ðær on innan giong
        niða nathwylc.

In some of these passages *þær* has, of course, the idiomatic
meaning 'when' (440, 1269, 775, etc.) or 'whereby' (1470): in
most, however, it has its usual sense, with an obvious antecedent.

27. Of *þonne* with conjunctive order there are only two exceptional instances in *Beowulf*, but these two are most instructive:

1104   Gyf þonne Frysna hwylc   frecnan spræce
        ðæs morþorhetes   myndgiend wære,
        þonne hit sweordes ecg   †syððan sceolde.

Here the first sentence is certainly subordinate to the second, but
it does not follow that the second is a principal sentence; the order
shows it is not. The first condition of Finn's pact was 'þæt ænig
mon wordum ne worcum wære ne bræce' and our text is the

second; it means 'if however any Frisian by reckless speech should revive the feud, [that] then sword-edge should settle it'; the head-word in 1106 is not 'þonne' but 'þæt' and the conjunctive order is therefore normal. The second instance is

2446   þonne he gyd wrece,
   sarigne sang, þonne his sunu hangað.

This again should not be printed as a principal sentence; the words preceding are 'swa bið geomorlic þæt his byre ride giong on galgan' and our text is a continuation, i.e. '[and that] he should then utter his grief when his son hangs on gallows and he may not help him'; the asyndeton in the co-ordinate clause is the rule in poetry as we shall see later. That this is the right interpretation is shown by the subjunctive 'wrece', parallel to 'ride' in the preceding clause; the reading 'wreceð', adopted by many editors, spoils both syntax and sense. On the other hand, in *Wulf* 9

  þonne hit wæs renig weder ond ic reotugu sæt
  þonne mec se beaducafa bogum bilegde
  wæs me wyn to þon wæs me hwæðre eac lað

the first line has no such justification for its order. The translation has 'it was rainy weather and I sat weeping when the man brave in battle gave me shelter'; if we place a colon at 'sæt', the *þonne*-sentences, arranged chiastically, are both subordinate, the first one to l. 8 Wulfes ic mines wenum dogode, and the second to l. 11; the general sense is 'my thoughts were ever on Wulf when it was rainy weather and I sat in tears, but when the warrior clasped me in his arms, it was so far pleasant, yet it was hateful too'.

28. We have still to enquire whether, in poetry as in prose, a sentence of the form 'þær (þonne) stod he' is ambiguous, i.e. may be either principal or subordinate; let us first consider sentences in which the verb is unstressed (e.g. wæs, wearð, sceal). Principal sentences, in which, of course, *þær* or *þonne* is the adverb, are quite common:

Beo.   847 Ðær wæs on blode brim weallende
    1745 Ðonne bið on hreþre under helm drepen...

The only comment on these is that the scansion proves, if there were any doubt on the point, that the adverb was stressed. Sub-

ordinate clauses with an unstressed verb appear to be disallowed
by all editors, although they admit such clauses with *þa*, e.g. 2372
bearne ne truwode ða wæs Hygelac dead: yet there are many
places where a subordinate clause yields excellent sense, e.g.

36	[mærne be mæste.]	Ðær wæs madma fela
89	[hludne in healle;]	þær wæs hearpan sweg
497	[hador on Heorote;]	þær wæs hæleða dream

in which *þær* cannot be the adverb (stressed) except on the assumption that a 3-lift *b*-verse was admissible. The subordinate character
of these sentences is certainly suggested by the analogy of similar
þa-clauses. Again, in

3051   þonne wæs þæt yrfe..., galdre bewunden

the editors' interpretation 'then, i.e. when the gold was hidden' is
disallowed by the sense, for temporal *þonne* could only be frequentative; it must here be a causal conjunction.

29. We must now consider the problem when the verb is stressed.
In dealing with *þa*-sentences of this kind (e.g. *þa com he*) comment
was made on the astonishing rarity in poetry of what is in prose
perhaps the most common of all sentence-forms. The rarity of
þær-sentences is even more remarkable: there is no example in
Beowulf, and only one, so far as I have observed, in the rest of OE
poetry, viz. *Maldon* 65:

[Ne mihte þær for wætere werod to þam oðrum;]
þær com flowende flod æfter ebban

Here a subordinate clause gives good sense, and sense is supported
by metre, for, if *þær* is the adverb, we have an unknown type of
half-line with four stresses. If the reader objects that this is to
overlook the possibility of *þær* being the unstressed expletive
adverb ('there came the flood-tide') it may be pointed out that this
explanation raises more problems than it solves; for in the late
prose writings in which expletive *þær* with a stressed verb occurs
it occurs repeatedly. If it was good usage in poetry why is it found
only once?

30. Rather more numerous are the *þonne*-sentences of the same form; we have in *Beowulf*

377   Ðonne sægdon þæt sæliðende
                 ...þæt he þritiges
            manna mægencræft on his mundgripe
            heaþorof hæbbe.

'Then sea-farers often said...' When? The adverb is meaningless in the context. If we take 'þonne sægdon' as a causal clause subordinate to the next sentence 381 hine halig God us onsende þæs ic wen hæbbe, we have good sense 'Since voyagers have said that he has the strength of thirty men, methinks God must have sent him to us against the terror of Grendel.'

525   Ðonne wene ic to þe wyrsan geþingea

The adverb is here not temporal, but means 'now' (*autem*) as in the instances from *Bede* discussed above, or possibly 'therefore'.

31. The examples in *Beowulf* being so few, let us consider some *þonne*-sentences from other poems; we have

Gen. 305.   [þær habbað heo on æfyn ungemet lange
               ealra feonda gehwilc fyr edneowe.]
               Ðonne cymð on uhtan easterne wind,
               forst fyrnum cald, symble fyr oððe gar.

This is a most instructive passage: it is supposed to mean 'at evening the fiends feel fire new-kindled; then comes at dawn an east wind, frost bitter-cold: always fire or piercing cold!' An exclamatory sentence, however, without finite verb, is not an OE idiom, yet 'fyr' certainly will not go with 'cymð on uhtan'. If we make 'þonne cymð' a subordinate clause, 'fyr', 'forst' and 'fyr oððe gar' all have a construction, i.e. as objects of 'habbað', and syntax and sense are good: 'where they feel at evening fire new-kindled, and at dawn, when the east wind comes, frost bitter-cold, always fire or frost'.

Wand. 45   ðonne onwæcneð eft wineleas guma,
               gesihð him biforan fealwe wægas...
               [Ðonne beoð þy hefigran heortan benne]

The correlation demands a clause instead of the first principal sentence and sense supports it; the poet has told us how the wanderer in his dream is once more in the gift-hall clasping and kissing his lord, but (he goes on) 'when he awakes [and] sees before him the dark seas, all the heavier are the wounds in his heart'. For the asyndetic clause see 85.

Best. B. 19   Ðonne gewiciað werigferhðe
on þæm ealonde, æled weccað...
hæleþ beoð on wynnum.

The editions make three principal sentences, but the meaning demanded by the context is 'when the weary ones are camped on the island [and] kindle fire, happy men are they'; the first two sentences are co-ordinate adverbial clauses after *þonne*. A word must be said about

Beo. 2041   þonne cwið æt beore seðe beah gesihð...

The line taken alone makes sense as a principal sentence, but is it credible that the poet began with 'þonne cwið' a sentence which he ends with 'ond þæt word acwið'? Moreover, 'þonne cwið' elsewhere is a dependent clause as in *Guth.* 4 ðonne cwið se engel, which is subordinate to Se bið gefeana fægrast, i.e. 'it is the fairest of joys when the angel says (to the happy soul)...'. In the *Beowulf* passage, however, a dependent clause is meaningless, and 'cwið' must be a misreading of some other word.

32. It would appear then that wherever *þær* and *þonne* are followed in poetry by a stressed verb, sense either forbids their being construed as adverbs or at least allows equally well of their being taken as conjunctions: conversely, wherever sense requires *þær* or *þonne* to be an adverb, each is invariably followed, not by a stressed verb, but by an unstressed one, as can be clearly seen in any pair of correlated sentences, e.g.

Beo. 2075   ðær we gesunde   sæl weardodon,
þær wæs Hondscio   hild onsæge.

484   Ðonne wæs þeos medoheal   on morgentid,
drihtsele dreorfah,   þonne dæg lixte.

33. At this point we naturally ask ourselves what are the sentence-forms with a stressed verb which in poetry take the place of the demonstrative type usual in prose. The same problem for *þa*-sentences was discussed in the last chapter, where it was shown that the regular forms in poetry are either 'Com þa' when the subject is not expressed or 'He þa' when for any reason the subject-pronoun has to be expressed.

We have just the same forms in þær- and þonne-sentences, and it will be well to give examples from a wide range of texts:

(i) Mald. 64   Ne mihte þær for wætere werod to þam oðrum
    Beo. 2460   Gewiteð þonne on sealman...
    Crist 1362   Onginneð þonne to þam yflum ungelice
                   wordum mæðlan
    Soul's Ad. 16 Cleopað þonne swa cearful...

(ii) Beo. 2385   He þær for feorme feorhwunde hleat
     Jud. 2   heo ðar þa gearwe funde
                   mundbyrd æt ðam mæran
     Wid. 66   me þær Guðhere forgeaf glædlicne maþþum
     Guth. 511   me þonne sendeð....

In the last two examples we have the governed pronoun standing first, as frequently with þa when the subject is not itself a personal pronoun. We surmised, both on metrical and other grounds, that in the 'com þa' form the adverb was enclitic and unstressed, whereas in the 'he þa' form the adverb had its usual stress and the pronoun was proclitic to it; and scansion leads us to the same conclusion about þær and þonne.

34. Our conclusions in this chapter are thus exactly the same, *mutatis mutandis*, as those which we quite independently reached regarding þa-sentences; they were summarised in 19 to which the reader is referred. The present chapter may be fitly brought to a conclusion by a brief restatement of the object and the method of our enquiry so far. The object has been to answer two closely related questions, viz. (i) whether sentences of the form 'þa (þær, þonne) he geseah' are possible principal sentences, as which they are frequently printed in modern editions, and (ii) whether sentences of the form 'þa (þær, þonne) geseah he', which are admittedly principal sentences as a rule, may also be subordinate. The method has been to take both kinds of sentence in texts translated from Latin and compare them with the Latin original, which has enabled us to answer confidently the first question in the negative and the second in the affirmative. We have then gone on

to examine supposed exceptions to our rules in texts which are not translations and to seek an alternative explanation of them; in these it has appeared that subordination, obligatory in the first kind of sentence and often preferable in the second, can be effected by a simple repunctuation of the text. We now proceed to consider some other kinds of adverbial clause.

CHAPTER IV

SENTENCES INTRODUCED BY *ÆR*, *FORÐAM*, *NU*, ETC.

35. Such words as *ær, forðam, nu, siððan, swa, þeah,* may (like *þa, þær, þonne*) be either adverbs or conjunctions; is there any way of distinguishing them? The question obviously only arises where they are head-words in a sentence, and it is quite clear from the usage of all OE prose (i) that as adverbs they are followed normally by common order, e.g. *Hom.* II. 376. 15 Ær he het faran to strætum ond to wicum: nu he het faran to wegum ond to hegum 'He had before commanded him to go to streets and lanes, now he commands him, etc.'; (ii) that as conjunctions they are followed either by conjunctive order or, especially when the finite verb is an auxiliary, by common order. It follows that a sentence like 'siððan he wæs on Brettanie gefaren' is ambiguous, i.e. can be either principal or subordinate, and there may be a momentary doubt as to the meaning when two such sentences are correlated; in *Hom.* II. 252 ft. Ær hi sind gebundene ær hi beon geborene 'They are bound before they are born', the mood, of course, is decisive. Ambiguous sentences are, however, not uncommon, and it is no doubt the desire to avoid ambiguity which accounts in such contexts for the occasional use of demonstrative order in the principal sentence, especially in the mature prose of Ælfric, e.g.

Hom. II. 166. 18. Ær se ærendraca mihte becuman ær hæfde he towend þone weall 'Before the messenger could arrive he had overthrown the wall'.

I. 304 ft. Siððan se geleafa sprang geond middangeard siððan geswicon þa wundra 'After the faith had spread all over the world miracles ceased';

and so in

Oros. 118. 11. Sona swa he gelacnad wæs swa hergeade he on Athene 'As soon as he had recovered he attacked Athens'.

36. The ambiguity is naturally a frequent source of mispunctuation in our printed texts. Two kinds of context in which this occurs may be specially mentioned.

(i) When the correlative adverb is expressed, e.g.

Oros. 14. 26. Nu hæbbe we scortlice gesæd ymbe Asia: nu wille we ymbe Europe londgemære areccan.

The Latin (Quoniam descripsimus) certifies the first sentence as subordinate: 'Now that we have briefly spoken about Asia we will go on to describe the boundaries of Europe.'

CP 108. 10. Forðon hit nas na gecweden ðæt hiene sceoldon oðre men ondrædan ac nietenu: forðon hit is ungecyndelicu ofermodgung...

So Sweet punctuates, making two principal sentences; the second *forðon* is a conjunction, and the meaning is 'The reason why it was said, not that other men should fear him, but beasts, is that it is unnatural pride (to wish to be feared by one's equals)'; this is good sense and what the argument demands. Instances are not uncommon in which the correlative adverb is unexpressed, e.g.

Oros. 58. 21. Nu we witon þæt ure Dryhten us gesceop: we witon eac þæt he ure reccend is 'Since we know that our Lord created us, we know also that he is our Ruler'.

and similarly in the two sentences which immediately follow it. In all, the semicolon should be a comma.

(ii) When a sentence, especially one introduced by *nu*, is followed by an imperative, e.g.

Oros. 80. 34. Nu we witan þæt we ure lif forlætan sceolan: uton þehhwæðre acræftan.... 'Since we know that we must leave this life, let us notwithstanding contrive...'

Hom. II. 426. 17. Nu we arison of deaðe and we lybbað. Stande nu þin cynedom on sibbe.... 'Since we have arisen from death and live, let thy Kingdom now stand in peace...'

Beo. 2646   Nu is se dæg cumen;...wutun gongan to
'Since the day is come, let us go to him'.

37. Most of these correlative words need no further comment, but *forðon* deserves a note to itself since the significance of correlation by means of this word is usually missed in our texts. When the principal sentence comes first, *forðon* (*forði*) shows that stress is laid not so much on the action predicated by the verb as on the reason for it (cf. the Latin Idcirco te defendi quia innocens eras 'My reason for defending you was that you were innocent'), e.g.

Blick. 3. 10. Forþon heo fæmne cende forðon heo wæs fæmne geeacnod 'The reason why she brought forth as a virgin was that she had conceived as a virgin'.

Hom. II. 278. 8. Ond forði ne sceal naðor buton oðrum beon geoffrod þæt Crist beo mid us ond we mid Criste 'The reason why neither must be offered without the other is so that Christ may be with us and we with Christ'.

Thorpe renders 'And therefore neither should be offered without the other, that...', which makes 'forði' refer to the preceding and not to the following sentence; and the same mistake is made by the *Blickling* translator. Another example of the construction is *CP* 108. 10 cited above. Instances in poetry are naturally rare but here is one from *Seafarer*:

58   Forþon nu min hyge hweorfeð ofer hreðerlocan
            ...Forðon me hatran sind
     Dryhtnes dreamas þonne þis deade lif

This should be punctuated as one sentence: the poet is explaining why his restless heart is always urging him to adventure and says that it is 'because the Lord's joys warm my breast more than this mortal life'. The first 'forðon' is an adverb, and the second a conjunction (unstressed since otherwise we have a 3-lift *b*-verse).

38. Before leaving these conjunctions it will be appropriate to mention a use of *þa* which is rarely allowed in our texts, viz. as a 'continuative' conjunction, e.g.

Oros. 174. 3. he gewicode neah anre ie seo wæs haten Bagrada: þa com of ðæm wætre an nædre (the Latin has *ubi* = when) 'He was encamped near a river called Bagrada when there came out of the water an adder'.

Hom. I. 60. 21. On ðam oðrum dæge eode se apostel be ðære stræt: þa ofseah he... 'On the second day he was going along the street when he saw...'.

II. 28. 22. on ærne-merien heo siðode swa swa heo gemynt hæfde. Ða geseah heo licgan ðone hring 'at daybreak she continued her journey as she had intended, when she saw the ring lying...'.

In each sentence replace the colon or full-stop by a comma. This is evidently the same construction as Latin *cum* with Indic., by which it may have been influenced since it is mostly confined to Ælfric and *Orosius*. It does not occur at all in poetry.

39. Conjunctive order after any of the words we are discussing is always, in prose, a certain indication of a subordinate clause; apparent exceptions are frequent especially in *Bede* (e.g. 148. 24 Swa hit gen to dæge Bretta þeaw is) but are invariably proved by the Latin to be, not principal sentences, but mispunctuated subordinate clauses. The usage of poetry will be discussed in 92.

40. Our conclusions in this chapter are that, when standing first in a sentence, any word (other than *þa, þonne, þær*) which in its written form may be either an adverb or a conjunction (i) is in prose invariably a conjunction if followed by conjunctive order, (ii) is ambiguous, i.e. may be either part of speech, both in prose and verse, when followed by common order. Demonstrative order is comparatively rare and is usually the mark of a principal sentence.

CHAPTER V

RELATIVE AND DEMONSTRATIVE PRONOUNS IN OLD ENGLISH

41. The simplest OE relative pronouns are *þe* and *se*, *þe* being used when the clause has the function of a limiting or distinguishing adjective and *se* when it has the function of a descriptive adjective, e.g. Se casere þe wæs Claudius haten 'the Emperor called Claudius', Se casere, se wæs Claudius haten 'the Emperor, who was called C.' In the first sentence the relative clause distinguishes one particular emperor from others, in the second it adds a descriptive detail to a noun already sufficiently defined by the context. Both kinds of clause may qualify the same noun, e.g. *Hom.* I. 100. 4 Se eahtateoða dæg þæs monðes þe we hataŏ Martius þone ge hataŏ Hlyda 'the 18th day of the month that we call March, which you call Hlyda'. The analogy of other subordinate clauses leads us to expect that conjunctive order will be the rule in the relative clause, and this we find to be the case; but common order is a frequent exception especially when the verb is unstressed, e.g. sum mæsse-preost on þam lande þe is gehaten Hispania se wæs ðearle geswenct. Occasionally the order of subject and verb is inverted as in *Hom.* II. 58. 25 Abel þone ofsloh Cain his broŏor.

42. In all the examples so far the antecedent has been a noun and the order of words in the principal sentence has presented no difficulty. The antecedent of the limiting relative pronoun may, however, be the demonstrative *se*, e.g. se biŏ cyning þe rixaŏ 'he that rules is King'; when this is the case, can any rule be laid down for the order of words in the principal sentence? The *Homilies* of Ælfric, our standard of mature OE prose, enable us to answer this question with complete certainty:

(i) If the pronoun-antecedent is the subject, it is followed immediately by the verb, e.g.

II. 410 ft. Se ðe wyrcð mines Fæder willan se færð into heofonan rice 'He that does my Father's will [he] goes into the Kingdom of Heaven'.

II. 374. 1. Se fandað þissera fif andgita seðe þurh fyrwitnysse hi aspent on unnyt 'That man tries the five senses who through curiosity wastes them uselessly'.

II. 48. 7. þa ðe Johannes fullode þa wæron eft gefullode 'Those that John had baptised were again baptised'.

(ii) If the pronoun-antecedent is in an oblique case, then (*a*) when the subject is a noun, we have demonstrative order, the verb standing next after the antecedent, e.g.

I. 138. 2. þone bær se ealda Symeon þe ealle ðing gewylt 'Simeon bore in his arms Him who rules all things'.

I. 184. 8. Ealle þa ðe him to cumað þa gesihð se Hælend 'All those that come to him the Saviour beholds'.

I. 190. 22. þæt ðe on him heora eagan gedydon þæt deð ure geleafa on us 'What their eyes did for them, that our faith does for us'.

(*b*) when the subject is a pronoun we have common order, e.g.

I. 282. 4. þæt þæt þu wylt þæt þu lufast 'that that thou willest thou lovest'.

I. 6. 5. þa ðe his leasungum gelyfað þam he arað 'those who believe in his lies he honours'.

II. 328. 22. þone ðe Drihten lufað þone he ðreað 'whom the Lord loveth he chasteneth'.

These rules are supported by every other OE text: exceptions like *Oros.* 56. 24 Gecwædon þæt þa ðe ær æt þæm aþum næren þæt þa ham gelendon 'that those not at the oath-taking should return home', are only apparent, since the conjunctive order of the last clause is determined by the conjunction *þæt*.

43. We have now to ask ourselves whether the rules still apply when the demonstrative pronoun is not an antecedent; in other words, can we detach the principal sentences in the passages cited and say (e.g.) þa wæron eft gefullode 'these were again baptised', þone bær se ealda Symeon 'him old Simeon bore', þam he arað to edleane 'these he honours as a reward'? Such principal sentences abound in all texts as printed, and it will be necessary to examine the evidence for them most carefully. Let us look at the supposed instances in texts which are translations and compare them with the Latin original:

(*a*) Principal sentences in which *se* (*seo, þa*), when not an antecedent, is the subject. There are in *Orosius* nineteen instances; in eight of these the Latin fails us, in the other eleven the Latin has either a relative clause or an adjectival phrase, e.g. apposition or participle, for which a relative clause is the usual OE equivalent (the antecedents are given in square brackets):

40. 17. [Se yldra wæs Danaus.] Se wearð of his rice adræfed and on Arge fleonde becom (Ipse Danaus, regno pulsus, Argos concessit)

78. 26. [Htesseus] Se wæs mid his dædum snelra þonne he mægenes hæfde (qui celeritate magis quam virtute fretus...)

82. 28. [Marðonius] Se hiene wæs georne lærende (Regem M. adgreditur, suadens...)

108. 16. [Minutia] Seo hæfde gehaten þæt heo wolde hire lif on fæmnhade alibban (The clause is a paraphrase of Virgo vestalis.)

164. 9. [Cartaina] Seo wæs getimbred fram Elisam (quae ab Elisa condita invenitur)

172. 6. [oþer consul wæs haten Cornelius:] se gefor on Liparis (C., consul alter, Liparam petiit)

292. 15. [Maximianus] Se wære wierðe Romana onwaldes (Augusto dignus)

22. 19. [Alpes] Ða onginnað fram þæm Wendelsæ (quae Gallico mari exsurgentes...)

114. 15. [On Tracia wæron twegen cyningas:] Ða wæron gebroþor (Cum eum fratres duo, Thraciae reges,...)

278. 15. [burga twa] Ða wæron on Tigris staðe (duas Parthorum urbes cepit super Tigridem)

288. 22. [þa Seaxan.] Ða wæron eardfæste neh þam garsecge (Saxones, gentem in Oceani litoribus sitam)

It is clear that every supposed principal sentence is really a relative clause; even where the Latin fails, a relative clause is always the construction which naturally suggests itself, e.g.

19. 19. [micel sæ]: seo is bradre þonne man oferseon mæge
192. 20. [Hasterbale] Se wæs eac Pena oþer cyning
72. 1. [hund monna]: þa wæron simbel binnan R. wuniende

What is remarkable in all these instances is that *se*, though taken by the editor as a demonstrative, never renders a Latin demonstrative pronoun; the reader must take it on trust that the same is true of the very numerous instances in *Bede*.

44. There are, however, in *Bede* rather frequent instances of a context (*ond se*) which might seem to certify the demonstrative sense of the pronoun because mere repunctuation is not enough to give the clause which it introduces an alternative meaning, e.g.

376. 31 he wæs mid adle gestanden and seo to þon swiðe weox. . . .
We have almost the same form of sentence in 382. 4, 392. 4, 462. 3;
in all but the last *seo* renders a Latin relative, and in two of them,
the first and third, one MS. either omits the *ond* or reads *ond heo*.
We have also 50. 3 and se mycele menigo heora fornom, and 148. 9
and se unrihtlice ofslegen wæs; for the first the Latin has 'quae
tantam multitudinem stravit', and in the second B omits the *se*.
In *ASC* we have:

716A. Her Osred wearð ofslegen and se hæfde VII winter rice
(where E omits the *and*)
755. butan anum gisle and se swiþe gewundad wæs (in all MSS.)

though just above (and se Cyneheard) E omits the conjunction.
Again, in Ælfric's *Pentateuch*, we have

Gen. xiv. 13. Ða ætbærst sum man and se hit sæde Abrame (*V.* Et
ecce unus qui evaserat nuntiavit Abram)
Gen. xli. 34. and se sette gerefan (*V.* qui constituat praepositos)

There is thus hardly a single instance of *ond se* which is not
suspect, and when we consider how easily the *ond*-sigil was
inserted or omitted, suspicion is increased.

45. There are also in *Bede* some half-dozen instances of another
strange use of *se*, in which the pronoun stands not at the head of
the sentence but within it, e.g.

100. 17. Ða se þa geseted wæs, B. þa se seonoð geset wæs (quod cum
esset statutum)
258. 29. wæs se asponen from Cent, B. se wæs, O. Ca. wæs he
(invitatus de Cantia)
326. 14. þa frægn hine se, (a quo interrogatus)
370. 23. wæs se in ealonde þæs meres, B. Ca. se in ealonde wæs (qui
in insula stagni. . .)
448. 17. þa se forðferde, (quo defuncto)

Some of these look like an attempt to render the Latin idiom by
which the relative pronoun can be the subject of an adverbial
clause (e.g. qui cum obiisset = after whose death) but neither the
Latin original nor the variant readings lend any support to the
view that *se* can be a demonstrative pronoun in a context where it
is not the antecedent. Those who hold this view have, moreover, a
difficult semantic problem to solve, viz. what is the difference in

meaning between *se* and *he*? It is a pertinent question, for there are many passages like the following:

Hom. II. 96. 19. He cuðe sumne man on Romebyrig....Se læg bedryda fram cildhade....He læg singallice and næfre sittan ne mihte.

LS 7. 10. ...wæs sum æðelboren mæden. Seo wan ðurh geleafan wið ða feondlican ealdras. Heo wæs wlitig on ansyne...

What is the distinction between *se* and *he* in the first passage, and between *seo* and *heo* in the second? If our reasoning has been correct, there is a syntactical difference, *se* and *seo* introducing a subordinate relative clause, and *he* and *heo* a principal sentence; and the punctuation should show this.

46. We go on to consider (*b*) supposed principal sentences introduced by oblique cases of the demonstrative pronoun. There are about 100 instances of these in *Bede*; for reasons of space I restrict myself to twenty of them which illustrate the pronoun in all cases and genders, assuring the reader that the remaining instances would only confirm the evidence of those cited. They include examples both of demonstrative and of common order (see 42 (ii) *a*, (ii) *b*) and I give in each case the opening words of the corresponding Latin sentence:

118. 25. Ðæm æfterfyligde Justus in biscophade (cui statim successit J.)

220. 13. Ðane cwom þider to halgianne Itthamar (quem ordinaturus venit...)

394. 16. Ðæs wif wæs mid adle gestanden (cuius conjux morbo...)

458. 5. Mid þone wæron cumende oþre bisceopas (cum quo et alii episcopi...)

476. 3. Æfter þam feng Aldwulf to þære ðenunge (post quem A. suscepit episcopatum)

478. 3. For þæm wæs ercebiscop geworden Tatwine (pro quo factus est T. episcopus)

The following all have common order:

154. 6. Ða com Eanfrid: þone he gelice hlete geniðrade (E. venientem simili sorte damnavit)

378. 2. Ðæs lichoman þa broðor... (Cujus corpus fratres...)

332. 17. : þære bysene heo wæs inhyrgende (cujus aemulata exemplum...)

210. 15. In þære (gesyhðe) he wæs monad (in qua admonitus est)

226. 26. In þæm he gesomnade micel weorod (in quibus collecto exercitu...)

298. 24. For þæm Theodor Q. gehalgode (pro quo consecravit...)

422. 8. Bi ðære se arwurða biscop cirican getimbrode (in quo aedificata ecclesia...)

In the next we have plurals with common or demonstrative order:

184. 10. : þara wæs oðer biscop in Lindesse (quorum prior in Lindissi provincia...)

306. 10. : þara se ærra wæs ofslegen (quorum prior occisus est)

378. 7. : þa sume we geara for gemynde awriton (e quibus aliqua memoriae mandavimus)

88. 31. In þæm wæron þa ærestan M. et J. (in quibus primi M. et J....)

346. 15. In eallum þæm he geornlice gemde (in quibus cunctis...)

214. 22. From þæm he manig þing gehyrde (a quibus non pauca audiit)

300. 9. Mid þæm wæs eac Eadhæd gehalgod (cum quibus et E. ordinatur)

It will be observed that in all but one of these passages the supposed OE demonstrative pronoun renders a Latin relative, and that in the one exception (154. 6 where the OE is turned differently) *þone* is most naturally construed as a relative pronoun.

47. We have reserved for separate consideration (*c*) the neuter pronoun *þæt*. It is used as a demonstrative in the nominative case in all the senses of ModE 'that', e.g.

Hom. I. 6. 26. Ic wille ofgan æt þe his blod þæt is his lyre 'I will require of thee his blood, that is his perdition.'

I. 42. 13. Ðæt is ece lif þæt hi þe oncnawon soðne God 'That is eternal life, to acknowledge thee as true God.'

There appears to be no reason why it should not be the subject of a stressed verb also; instances are rare, and it is remarkable that whenever it can be tested in texts translated from Latin it renders the relative pronoun. In *Bede* 200. 28 Ðæt gelomp in þa tid þætte Penda... its obvious construction is as a relative after 'oðer wundor' in the preceding sentence: 'another marvellous event which happened at this time, viz. that Penda, etc.' Let us now turn to the oblique cases of *þæt*. Of the accusative there are in *Bede* and *Orosius* ten instances in which the pronoun is the head-word, but in all but three the Latin fails. Two of these three have

what looks like the appropriate demonstrative order (42. (ii) a) viz.
Oros. 172. 2 Ðæt gefremede Duulius hiora consul, Bede 374. 15
Ðæt wolde ða æteawan seo godcunde arfæstnes; in the first the
Latin has 'quod D. consul implevit', in the second, since the words
begin a new chapter, þæt is meaningless either as demonstrative or
relative. The Latin has 'volens autem', and one MS. reads 'Ða
wolde þa' which is obviously correct: 'Since the Divine providence
wished to show....' In the third instance we have the common
order usual with a pronoun-subject (42. (ii) b), but the Latin disallows the demonstrative pronoun: Oros. 60. 8: þæt ic wille eac
gescadwislecor gesecgean (quod utrum ita sit apertissime ex-
pediam). We have an apparent instance of the same order in Gen.
xxxvii. 22 þæt he sæde forðam ðe he wolde, etc., where the Vulgate
has Hoc dicebat: here þæt may be a misreading of þes, since 'þes he
sæde' is the usual rendering of the Latin phrase. Of the genitive
þæs instances are rare except in the phrase 'þæs is to tacne' (Bede
264. 11); by contrast with 'þæs to tacne is' (116. 16) this looks like
a principal sentence 'of this we have a proof', but the Latin for
both forms alike is invariably denique and the relative pronoun
always gives an appropriate sense in both.

48. We can now summarize our conclusions so far. No part of
the demonstrative pronoun se seo þæt other than the neuter
nominative can stand at the head of a sentence except as antecedent, and any supposed instance to the contrary is really a
relative pronoun.

49. A simple repunctuation will usually make faulty sentences
regular and it will be appropriate, since we have used translated
texts to prove our rule, to illustrate from other texts the kind of
remedy just mentioned:

Hom. II. 66. 22. Babilonia is gereht gescyndnys. Seo getacnað helle
'B. is interpreted "confusion", [which] betokens hell'.

II. 296 ft. Se apostel hæfde twa dohtra. Ða þurhwunodon on
mægðhade 'The apostle had two daughters, [who] continued in
virginity'.

II. 516. 5. ...preostas; ða he wolde sibbian ær his forðsiðe 'priests,
[whom] he wished to reconcile before his death'.

l. 532 ft. ...sum broðor. Ðam filigde sum flæslic broðor 'a monk,
[who] was followed by a certain carnal brother'.

It will not be amiss to classify the contexts in which this kind of mispunctuation is most frequent:

(i) The double relative clause. When the *se*-clause comes first, e.g. Is þæt þæt mynster, þæt is nu micel of medmiclum gefremed, þe gewunelice is Mingeo nemned 'this is the abbey, now greatly enlarged, that is usually called Mingeo', the syntax is unmistakeable and the pointing correct; it is when the *se*-clause comes second that mispunctuation often occurs, e.g.

Hom. I. 258. 10. he geceas ða twelf leorning-cnihtas þe we apostolas hatað. Ða wæron mid him æfre siððan 'He chose the twelve that we call apostles, [who] were ever afterwards with him'.

Oros. 19. 7. ...to þæm porte þe mon hæt æt Hæþum: se stent betweoh Winedum ond Seaxum 'to the port called Heathby, [which] stands between the Wends and the Saxons'.

Both relative clauses may be descriptive if sense requires, e.g.

ASC 890. Goðrum þæs fulluht-nama wæs Æþelstan se wæs Ælfredes godsunu 'Guthrum, Alfred's godson, who had been baptised A.'

Hom. II. 18. 26. ðry cnihtas: þa wæron gehatene Annanias Azarias Misahel. Ða gecwædon... 'Three young men [called] Ananias, Azarias and Misael, [who] resolved...'

(ii) When the clause follows an interrogative sentence, e.g.

Hom. I. 264. 11. Hwæt is þæt rice buton ða halgan menn þe he alysde fram hellewite? Ða he betæcð his agenum Fæder 'What is the Kingdom but the holy men that he redeemed from hell-torment, [whom] he will deliver to his Father?'

II. 280. 15. Hwæt is þæs lambes innewerde buton Cristes bebodu? ða we etað þonne we lifes word underfoð 'What is the lamb's inward part but Christ's commands, [which] we eat when we receive the word of life?'

(iii) Sentences introduced by the indefinite neuter *þæt*. If the sentence comes first it is, as a rule, unmistakeably a relative clause, e.g.

Hom. I. 318. 26. ond eac, þæt wundorlicor wæs, ælcum wæs geþuht swilce he spræce mid his gereorde 'and further, what was more wonderful, he seemed to everyone to be speaking in his own language'.

If it comes last, it is usually punctuated by editors as a principal sentence, e.g.

Oros. 172. 2. Ðæt Duulius heora consul gefremede 'which [i.e. the building of a fleet] the consul D. accomplished'.

Hom. I. 496 ft. He mæg ða synfullan sawle geliffæstan. Ðæt ge-swutelode se Hælend þaþa he þæt mæden arærde 'He can quicken the sinful soul, [as] the Saviour made clear when he raised the maiden'.

I. 548. 23. Sittende he tæhte: þæt belimpð to wurðscipe lareow-domes 'sitting he taught, [an attitude which] befits the magisterial dignity'.

Blick. 123 mid. Ðæs we sceolon Drihtne þanc secgan 'for all [which] we ought to thank the Lord'.

50. There are, however, certain adverbs and adverbial phrases, pronominal in origin, to which our rule does not apply, no doubt because the pronoun had ceased to be felt as such, e.g. *forðam* 'therefore', *ðæs* 'after'. These may stand as adverbs at the head of a sentence, as in *ASC* 871 Ðæs ymb iv niht 'four days after'. Since the pronominal element in such words may be a relative, they can also, of course, be used as conjunctions, *forðam* 'because', *ðæs* 'since', e.g. *ASC* 894 ymb twelf monað þæs hie comon 'twelve months after they had arrived'. *Bi ðam*, on the other hand, appears to be used not as an adverb but only as a conjunction ('as'), e.g. *Hom.* I. 322. 30 todælende æghwilcum be ðam ðe him gewyrð 'assigning to every man as seems to him good'. It is common in the *Homilies* and *CP* in sentences like Bi ðam Johel se witga cwæð 'as Joel the prophet spake' introducing a quotation from Scripture. In these it is usually rendered 'concerning this (or these)', a literal analysis not supported by the analogy of other similar phrases and disallowed by our rule; there is, of course, no objection to its retaining its full force as a *relative* pronoun in a proper context, e.g. þa fule leahtras be ðam cwæð se apostel 'the foul sins of which the Apostle spake'.

51. We have reached the conclusions that the nominative *se* (*seo*) is never demonstrative except as antecedent, that the nomi-native *þæt* is freely used even when it is not the antecedent, and that, with the exception mentioned in 50, any oblique case of the demonstrative pronoun cannot stand *first* in a sentence unless it is the antecedent. Internally, however, the oblique cases in all genders are used freely, e.g.

Hom. II. 18. 15. An ðæra wæs Sibylla 'One of these (heathen witnesses) was the Sibyl'.

II. 480. 26. Sy þæs Gode lof 'Praise be to God for that'.

II. 294 ft. Arærað Cristes rode and gebiddað eow to ðære 'Raise up Christ's rood and pray to that'.

II. 210. 21. Hi offrodon lamb ond he wæs eac on ðam getacnod 'They offered a lamb and he was also symbolised by that'.

The doxologies in the *Homilies* are a *locus classicus* for the distinction between front position and internal position, e.g. demonstratives II. 528 us getiðað þæs, II. 472 sy him þæs wuldor; relatives II. 332 þæs us getiðige, I. 76 þæs him sy wuldor (which latter Thorpe translates also as demonstratives). Since *heora* in prose always precedes the word on which it depends, e.g. heora an, heora oðer, we have the interesting series:

(i) *Oros.* 88. 19. Heora an wæs Claudius haten (Personal Pn.)
(ii) *Hom.* II. 482. 13. An þara hatte Simon (Dem. Pn.)
(iii) *Bede* 184. 10. Ðara wæs oðer biscop (Rel. Pn.)

i.e. (i) 'one of them', (ii) 'one of these', (iii) 'one of whom'. The translators wrongly give 'one of whom', 'of these one', for the last two.

52. Supposed exceptions to our rule abound in verse; from considerations of space we confine our attention to *Beowulf* and to those instances in the punctuation of which all the modern editions are agreed:

(i) *Se* is made the demonstrative where it is not an antecedent:

196	[Higelaces þegn] Se wæs moncynnes mægenes strengest
898	[Wælses eafera] Se wæs wreccena wide mærost
1296	[anne] Se wæs Hroðgare hæleþa leofost
2024	[dohtor Hroðgares] Seo gehaten is suna Frodan
2087	[glof] Sio wæs orðoncum eall gegyrwed
2391	[god cyning] Se ðæs leodhryres lean gemunde
3042	[legdraca] Se wæs fiftiges fotgemearces.

These are all relative clauses, the antecedents being given in brackets; two of them (2024, 2391) have conjunctive order and must in any context be clauses. Immediately after 898 we have the sentence 'he þæs aron ðah'; if *se* is a demonstrative pronoun, why the change to *he*?

(ii) An oblique case standing first is made a demonstrative, e.g.:

12	[god cyning] Ðæm eafera wæs æfter cenned
59	[Healfdene] Ðæm feower bearn...in woruld wocun
1037	[mearas] Ðara anum stod | sadol searwum fah

1145   [hildeleoman] þæs wæron mid Eotenum ecge cuðe
1349   [ellorgæstas] ðæra oðer wæs | idese onlic
2194   [sincmaððum] Ðæt [? þe] he on Beowulfes bearm alegde
2769   [segn eallgylden] of ðam leoma stod
3014   [beagas] þa sceal brond fretan.

These again are relative clauses: all except two have conjunctive order.

(iii) *þæt* (nominative) is made a demonstrative when not followed immediately by the verb:

1255   Ðæt gesyne wearð
2327   Ðæt ðam godan wæs
        hreow on hreðre
2709   Ðæt ðam þeodne wæs
        siðast sigehwil

The conjunctive order stamps all these as subordinate clauses of some kind 'so that it was seen', etc. In others the presence of an obvious antecedent points to the pronoun being the relative even when the order allows the demonstrative, e.g.

309   [sæl timbred;] þæt wæs foremærost | receda
454   [hrægla selest.] Ðæt is Hrædlan laf
1559   [eald sweord.] þæt wæs wæpna cyst
1548   [breostnet broden;] þæt gebearh feore

The last is the only instance in the poem of a stressed verb following *þæt*.

(iv) *þæt* (acc.) or *þæs*, when the head-word, is taken as the demonstrative, e.g.

194   Ðæt fram ham gefrægn Higelaces þegn
588   þæs þu in helle scealt
        werhðo dreogan
942   Hwæt! þæt secgan mæg
        efne swa hwylc mægþa swa þone magan cende
2479   Ðæt mægwine mine gewræcan
2629   ne his mæges laf
        gewac æt wige;   þæt se wyrm onfand.

Only in 942 is *þæt* a demonstrative; here, however, *hwæt* is the head-word and it is followed, as always in the poem, by conjunctive order. In 194 sense disallows even a relative since the line begins a new paragraph; *þæt* is a scribal error, as elsewhere, for *þa*, which gives excellent sense 'when in his home afar he heard of Grendel's

deeds, he bade prepare a goodly ship'. In the other passages *þæt*
is the usual indefinite neuter, 'for which (i.e. the slaying of thy
brother) thou must suffer damnation (588)', 'which (i.e. their
plotting of forays) my kinsmen avenged (2479)', 'which (i.e. that
the sword did not fail him) the dragon discovered'. In the last
passage '*þa*' is the MS. reading, and '*swa*' would be a better
emendation.

53. A word must be said about the sentence-form Ðæt wæs god
cyning, usually treated as exclamatory 'That was a good king!'.
In this context, however, *þæt* means 'such a one' as defined by an
adjacent clause; in 11 and 2390 it is followed by the lines cited
above, Ðæm eafera wæs æfter cenned, and Se ðæs leodhryres lean
gemunde, the conjunctive order of which marks them as subordinate clauses, and the sense is 'A good king was he, to whom in
after days a son was sent by God to solace his people' and 'A good
king was he, who remembered to avenge his lord's downfall'; in
each case the relative clause defines the demonstrative pronoun.
In other contexts where a defining clause is lacking, e.g.

1075		hie on gebyrd hruron
	gare wunde;	þæt wæs geomuru ides.
1812		nales wordum log
	meces ecge.	Ðæt wæs modig secg

(usually rendered 'That was a sad lady!', 'That was a proud man!')
the sentences are more naturally taken as consecutive clauses:
'fated they fell by the spear, so that a sad lady was the Queen',
'he belittled not the blade, and a proud man was Unferth'.

54. The usual position in poetry of the neuter demonstrative in
any oblique case is after the subject-pronoun or, if the subject is
not a pronoun, after a governed pronoun, e.g.

632	Ic þæt hogode þa ic on holm gestah
	'This was my purpose when I put out to sea'
798	Hie þæt ne wiston
7	he þæs frofre gebad
1774	Me þæs on eþle edwenden cwom
	'All that was changed for me'

The pronoun was, no doubt, proclitic to the stressed demonstrative
as in 'he þa', 'he þær', etc., already discussed. The reader will

observe that the order Ðæt ic hogode (632) or Ðæt hie ne wiston (798) would be equally regular metrically, and the fact that it never occurs is a further argument that it was not good usage. The only lines in which *þæt* (acc.) is the head-word are

1700	Ðæt la mæg secgan se þe soð ond riht fremeð on folce
2864	Ðæt la mæg secgan se wyle soð specan

where the exceptional position of the pronoun is, no doubt, due to the *la*, since interjections always influence word-order. We conclude that, except for the sentence-forms mentioned in this paragraph, the rules governing the syntax of the demonstrative pronoun when not the antecedent are the same in poetry as in prose.

55. We have not discussed in this chapter the problem of a demonstrative pronoun, not the antecedent, followed by conjunctive order, since that order is never found after the demonstrative as antecedent. Instances, however, are numerous in our texts as printed, e.g.:

Bede 40. 13. Be þam þonne cuð is
    46. 5. Ðone man nu todæg sceawian mæg
    50. 14. Ðæt cuð is
    92. 4. Se Bretta þeode fornom

Comparison with the Latin shows that every such sentence is the subordinate clause which the word-order leads us to expect, and that the supposed demonstrative is therefore, here as elsewhere, a relative pronoun.

CHAPTER VI

SOME SYNTACTICAL GROUPS IN OLD ENGLISH

56. In a principal sentence the normal position of personal pronouns is next to the verb, either before or after, e.g. ic wene 'I think', ne wene ic 'I do not think', us sæde se halga Beda 'the holy Bede has told us', him wæs metes micel lust 'he was inordinately hungry'. If there are two or more pronouns they usually stand together, e.g. ic hit eom 'it is I', ic þe þancige 'I thank thee', ne cann ic eow 'I know you not', þa forlet he hine 'he then left him', though they may be separated by the verb, e.g. ic þancige þe, heo offrað him gold. In sentences like 'þa forlet se deofol hine' (instead of 'þa forlet hine se deofol') the subject, though a noun, has asserted its priority over the pronoun-object: and so in *ASC* 921 Ða gegaderode micel folc hit 'a great host gathered', *Hom.* II. 104. 27 Ne forlæt se Ælmihtiga þe 'the Almighty will not forsake thee'. This order is rare. Contrariwise, in conjunctive sentences, where the pronouns usually stand apart from the verb, the pronoun-object is sometimes attracted by the verb, e.g. ac he for us eallum to deaðe hine sealde 'but he gave Him over to death for us all', *Hom.* II. 450. 24 Drihten me forgeaf þa æhta ond Drihten hi me eft benam 'the Lord gave me the possessions and the Lord has taken them away'. The order in this last clause is no doubt due to the stress on Drihten. Occasionally the pronoun-object follows the verb as it may do in the principal sentence, e.g. *Matt.* v. 11 þonne hi wyriað eow and ehtað eow 'when they curse you and persecute you', which may have been influenced by *V.* Cum maledixerint vobis: but in some of the instances, where a particular stress is required, the order is no doubt significant, e.g.

Hom. I. 242. 26. Ic lufige hi ond hi lufiað me 'I love them and they love mé'.

II. 234. 6. He wuldrað his Fæder ond se Fæder wuldrað hine 'He glorifies his Father and his Father hím'.

II. 524. 22. Ne gecure ge me ac ic geceas eow, 'Ye did not choose me but Í chose yóu'.

In all such instances of broken order, however, the pronoun is not separated from the verb, and there must be something wrong with

Beo. 932   Ðæt wæs ungeara þæt ic ænigra me
             Weana ne wende...

where the normal order 'þæt ic me ænigra' (as in 1772) restores the metre; syntactical usage would similarly disallow the suggested emendation *hit* for *his*, at least with the same order, in

2481   þeah ðe oðer his   ealdre gebohte.

There is, of course, nothing unusual in

946   Nu ic, Beowulf, þec,
       secga betsta, me for sunu wylle...

since the vocatives, as always, stand outside the structure of the sentence (Nu ic þec me...wille).

57. Personal pronouns governed by prepositions, being disjunctive, are naturally not subject to the pronoun-rule and often stand apart from the verb, e.g. He ableow sawle on him 'He breathed a soul into him', *Deut.* xxxii. 23 Ic gegadrie yfelu ofer hig ond afastnie mina flana on him 'I will heap evil on them and will fasten my arrows in them'. There is, however, an idiomatic inversion which often serves to give the pronoun its regular place in the sentence, e.g. Him com to Godes engel ond him sawle on ableow, *Hom.* II. 470 ft. Ne clypað he ða him to ðe hi sylfe rihtwise taliað 'He calls not to him those who count themselves righteous'. In expressions like Him to wurðmynte and us to beterunge 'for his honour and our improvement' the dative pronoun depends on the noun and is idiomatically used in such contexts instead of the possessive: so in

Hom. I. 106. 7. ða apostolas þe Crist geceas of Judeiscum folce us to hyrdum and to lareowum 'whom Christ chose as our shepherds and teachers'.

It is a mere accident if the pronoun in this construction stands next to the verb, as in

Hom. I. 44. 3. ðam ðingum ðe he gefremode us to alysednysse and to ecere blisse 'the things that he has done for our redemption and our eternal bliss'.

58. When the subject is a noun, the verb often stands first, e.g. Weox dæghwonlice Godes bodung 'The preaching of God increased daily', Wæs Breotene ealond Romanum uncuð 'The island of Britain was unknown to the Romans', and occasionally when the subject is a stressed pronoun, e.g. *Oros.* 118. 6 Wæs þæt micel wundor þæt eall Persa anweald... 'It was a great wonder that the whole power of Persia, etc.' Normally, however, the subject-pronoun must precede its verb in an affirmative sentence. This is the rule in Ælfric and in OE prose generally; in poetry inversion sometimes occurs when the verb is a stressed one, e.g. *Beo.* 590 Secge ic þe to soðe, 728 Geseah he in recede. In the Alfredian translation of *Bede*, however, the inverted order is frequent, not only when the verb is stressed but even when it is unstressed; there are in fact many pages on which there is a sequence of such sentences, e.g. 194. 6 Wæs he Osrices sunu.... Wæs he seofon winter cyning.... Wæs he se mon æfæst ond arfæst..., and there is hardly a paragraph without Cwæð he, frægn he, andswarode he. The order occurs occasionally in *Blickling* also. It might appear that 'cwæð he' is the ancestor of ME quoth he; this, however, is dubious, as it is almost entirely confined to *Bede*, and Ælfric always has He cwæð.

59. Inversion is, of course, the rule after demonstrative adverbs (4), in negative sentences (Chap. VII), and in questions and commands, e.g. Agif þu þine hond; Hwæt secge ge þæt ic eom? An instance like *Hom.* II. 322. 1 Ge manna bearn, demað rihtlice 'Ye sons of men, judge aright' is no exception since the pronoun goes with the vocative. Except in such a context, front position of the pronoun in a command or question is always a certain mark of the co-ordinate clause, e.g.

Hom. II. 296. 4. Far to westene...and þu nanum men ne drece 'Go to the wilderness and trouble thou no man'.

Deut. xiii. 8. Ne hire þu him ne þu him ne ara 'Hearken thou not to him nor spare thou him'.

Hom. I. 480. 6. Eart þu se ðe toweard is oððe we oðres anbidian sceolon? 'Art thou he that cometh or must we look for another?'

II. 108. 10. Hwænne gesawe we þe hungrine and we þe gereordodon? 'When saw we thee hungry and we fed thee?'

There is, therefore, something wrong with

Beo. 1170   þu on sælum wes

where the position both of pronoun and verb points to a co-ordinate clause: *ond* must have been omitted (cf. 1488 ond þu Hunferð læt ealde lafe habban).

60. There are some exceptions to the rule which are easily explicable, e.g.

Hom. I. 314. 20. La hwæt þis beon sceolde? 'Lo! what might this be?'
LS 23. 532. La hwæt þis æfre beon scyle...?
23*b*. 667. Eala hwæðer heo hider cumende syo? 'Alack! is she coming hitherwards?'

The conjunctive order in all these is the regular one in a sentence introduced by an interjection. After *hwæðer*, however, it is found without interjection in all prose writings, and it will be well to illustrate it rather fully:

Hom. I. 136. 30. Hwæðer ic mote lybban oðþæt ic hine geseo? 'Can I possibly live until I see him?'
Oros. 220. 8. Hwæðer Romane hit witen ænigum to secganne? 'Do the Romans know it so as to tell it to any man?'
CP 116. 9. Hwæðer ic cume þe mid ege þe mid lufe? 'Shall I come with terror or with love?'
Matt. xx. 15. Hwæðer þe þin eage manful ys...? 'Is thine eye evil...?'
John iv. 33. Hwæðer ænig man him mete brohte? 'Has any man brought him aught to eat?'
Gen. xxxi. 14. Hwæðer wit ænig þing agon of uncres fæder æhton? 'Have we any portion in our father's possessions?'

These questions are usually of the type which implicitly rejects the answer Yes; the Latin original, where there is one, has *an* or *num*. Syntactically, they all have the appearance of a subordinate clause, and the subjunctive mood, usually marking a dependent question, is noteworthy in some of them; the best parallel to them seems to be the Latin single question introduced by *an*. In *Blick.* 155 ft., however, 'Hwæt wille ge nu? Hwæt ic hine doo?' the second *hwæt* can only be a scribal error for *þæt*.

61. We shall now consider a problem of word-order in the syntactical combination subject-pronoun + verb in an affirmative principal sentence. We have seen that in such a sentence the pronoun is proclitic to the verb (a noun-subject may, of course, stand apart from it, e.g. Se Hælend ða untrumme gehælde) and that the separation of the two is normally only found in a conjunctive sentence, i.e. a subordinate or co-ordinate clause. Are there any conditions in which such separation can occur in a principal sentence? We confine ourselves for the present to instances where the pronoun is the head-word. Sweet lays down the rule (*Syntax*, p. 15) that 'even full nouns may occasionally have the same position' (i.e. between the subject-pronoun and the verb); this is not true in the general sense which he seems to imply, but only in a few particular contexts.

62. There are certain classes of words which OE idiom allows to be attached to the pronoun or prefixed to the verb and thus to separate the pronoun from the verb:

(i) An adjective, usually numerical, may further define the pronoun (we ðry, hi ealle, ic sylf), e.g.:

Hom. I. 200 ft. Hi butu wæron rihtwise 'They were both righteous'.
II. 318. 2. Ge ealle sind gebroðra and ænne Fæder habbað 'Ye are all brothers and all have one Father'.
Blick. 13. 13. heo sylf hie þeowen nemde 'she herself called herself handmaid'.

More usually *ealle* stands before the pronoun except in the clause, e.g.

Hom. I. 54. 8. Ealle we sind gebroðra...and we ealle cweðað 'We are all brothers and we all say...'

(ii) A noun defines the pronoun, e.g. we menn, ge wifa,

Hom. II. 390. 26. We strange sceolon beran þæra unstrengra byrðene 'We strong ones should bear the burden of the weak'.

It will be observed that in most examples so far the verb comes immediately after the interposed adjective or noun. In the following the disturbance is greater and the order may even be completely conjunctive.

(iii) An adverb intervenes, e.g.

Hom. II. 96 ft. He symle on his legere Gode ðancode 'He ceaselessly thanked God on his sick-bed'.
Bede 260. 5. Ic lustlice from þære þegnunge gewite 'I cheerfully resign the bishopric'.
Hom. II. 512. 21. He nateshwon ne ondred hiora deofollican hiw 'He nowise dreaded their devilish aspect'.
Bede 440. 10. Heo instæpe from minre gesihðe geweoton 'They immediately vanished from my sight'.

This is evidently the ancestor of the ModE order, but in OE it occurs only in elevated prose. The expression He soðlice 'but he', frequent in the Gospels, is not OE idiom but a Latinism rendering *Ille vero* and the like; Ælfric, however, uses it on occasion, e.g.

Hom. I. 462. 12. wendon þæt se deað hine gehæftan mihte: he soðlice ðone deað oferswyðde 'They thought that death might hold him captive: but he overcame death',

perhaps quoting the Scripture.

(iv) With demonstratives. The forms 'he þa' 'he þæt' 'he þær' have been sufficiently illustrated in verse; in prose only 'he þa' is common, though all occur, e.g.

Hom. I. 116. 2. Hi þa mid astrehtum lichaman hi to Criste gebædon 'They then with prostrate bodies prayed to Christ'.
Judg. xv. 13. Hie þa hine gebundon mid twæm bæstenum rapum 'They then bound him with two ropes of bast'.
Oros. 76. 7. Him þær se geonga cyning þæs oferfæreldes forwiernan mehte 'There the young king might have prevented his crossing'.
Hom. I. 464. 25. He þærrihte ut gewat 'He straightway went out'.
CP 26. 20. Hi þonne se ecea and se digla dema upahefð 'Then the eternal secret judge shall raise them up'.

In these, as in the examples already given from verse, it will be observed that conjunctive order is the rule. The form 'he þæt', which in verse is the most common of all, is in prose the rarest; it only seems to occur in *Orosius*, e.g. 44. 15 Hie þæt gelæstan swa, 72. 34 He þæt mid dædum gelæste 'He followed up his words with deeds': *ond* may have been omitted in these two sentences.

63. So far the unstressed character of the pronoun has not been affected; we shall now consider some contexts in which it is.

Whenever a proper noun follows the subject-pronoun, it has a suspensive effect which itself confers a stress, e.g.

Oros. 284. 14. He Constantinus hit hæfde XXIIII wintra 'Hé, Constantine, held it for twenty-four years'.

Hom. II. 434. 10. Ic Nabochodonosor ahof mine eagan up to heofonum 'Í, Nebuchadnessar, lifted up mine eyes to heaven'.

And so often in Charters and Laws 'ic Æðelfrið', 'ic Ine mid Godes gife cyning'. Some adverbs in this position point to a stress, even if they do not confer it; the most noteworthy of these stress-pointing words is *ærest (swiðost, fyrmest)*, e.g.

Bede 410. 21. Hé ærest getimbrede and gestaðolede þæt minster in Hi 'Hé was the first to build and found the monastery on Iona'.

LS 23. 363. Hí swiðost ælces gedweldes tiledon 'Théy more than any others gave themselves to every heresy'.

Bede 100. 31. Foreseoð ge þæt hé ærest to þære seonoðstowe cume 'Take care that hé is the first to enter the assembly-room'.

By contrast we have the order, when the stressed word is a noun,

Oros. 276. 2. Ærest Germanie þe be Donua wæron forhergedon Italiam 'It was the Germans on the Danube that first harried Italy'.

We have, therefore, the series

Ærest Críst dumbe ond deafe gehælde 'Chríst was the first...',
Hé ærest dumbe ond deafe gehælde 'Hé was the first...',
Ærest he gehælde dumbe ond deafe 'First he healed...',

the meaning in the last sentence being that the healing of the deaf and dumb was his first act; it is the regular order for this sense, e.g. *Hom.* I. 320. 10 Ærest he wolde us mid liðnysse styran þæt he siððan mihte on his dome us gehealdan 'he would first direct us by gentleness that he might afterwards preserve us at his judgement'. In this last type the pronoun has, of course, no stress.

64. A personal pronoun, when stressed in its own right, enjoys all the freedom of a noun and, like a noun, may be widely dissociated from its verb. Such separation is chiefly confined to verse, and it has been a mark of poetic idiom in all periods of English: examples will be given later from OE poetry, and it will suffice here to give a well-known one from Milton:

> So hé with difficulty and labour hard
> Moved on.

In prose this interception of the pronoun has not been common at any period and in OE is hardly to be found outside the pages of Ælfric. We begin with an instructive example:

Hom. II. 138. 20. Ic ðinum gedwylde dearnunge miltsige, gif þu ða gesihðe mid swigan bediglast 'Í thine error will privily condone if thóu in silence pass over that sight'.

This is from one of the alliterative, and therefore somewhat poeticised, homilies; the scansion makes it quite clear that the two subject-pronouns (*ic* and *þu*) are stressed since otherwise we have two short verses. The next example is from a non-alliterating homily:

Hom. I. 72. 15. Gif þu on God gelyfan wylt, ic unforhtmod ðæs drences onfo 'If thóu wilt believe in God, Í unafraid will receive this drink',

but here also the strong contrast of the pronouns marks them both as stressed. An example of a different kind is

Hom. I. 426. 9. Ic on mines Drihtnes naman nateshwon ne forhtige for ðinum tintregum 'I, in the name of my Lord, am nowise afraid of thy tortures'.

The stress on the pronoun here is due to the suspensive effect of the words following. In II. 282. 26 He us gelæde to his Lifigendan Fæder 'May Hé lead us to his living Father' it is the natural stress on 'he' which justifies the departure from the normal order (in a wish-sentence) Gelæde he us. We have sometimes a disjunctive pronoun in a context where the verb is unexpressed: this, of course, is always stressed, e.g. na hé swaðeah ac Crist 'yet not hé, but Christ'; *Hom.* II. 500. 9 ðam he sylf þenode swa swiðe swa hé hím, 'whom he served as devotedly as the other did hím'.

65. Let us now look at some instances of interception in which sense disallows a stress to the pronoun and see if we can find some other explanation of them. We begin with the five examples from *Orosius*, in which text they are fairly common:

46. 16. Hie heora here on tu todældon.
68. 20. [and hie begeaton þær Mucius nære:] he hi mid his wordum geegsade ['they would have captured it had it not been for Mucius:] he overawed them with his words'.

76. 27. Hio mid þæm healfan dæle farende wæs 'She went on with half of the army'.

82. 23. hi him þære bene getygðedon 'they granted them their request'.

134. 4. He hie to gewildum gedyde 'He reduced them to subjection'.

Failing a stress on the pronoun, the conjunctive order in all these points to some kind of clause; in the first the Latin has *'quae agmine diviso'*, in the last two C, the better MS., begins the sentences with *ond*; in 76. 27 since the sentence before has described the division of the army, Orosian idiom leads us to expect Hio þa (it occurs twice on the same page) 'She then went on'; 'geegsade' in 68. 20 can only be co-ordinate to 'nære' (the Latin has 'nisi hostem...permovisset) and *ne* may have been omitted before 'he' (73). Here are two examples from *Bede*:

44. 11. onsendon ærendwrecan to Rome mid gewritum ond wependre bene: him fultumes bædon (So M.).

Remove the colon and put a comma after 'gewritum' and we have a good sentence 'sent messengers with letters, and with piteous appeals begged for help'.

124. 12. he sigefæst swa eft ham ferde 'he thus returned home victorious'.

A good MS. has 'ond he sigefæst...' which makes the syntax regular. There is no indubitable instance of the anomaly in Ælfric, for in

Hom. II. 30. 23. Witodlice se ylca deofol ðe hi ær tihte, se hi eft siððan to hire agenre hengene gelærde 'Verily! the same devil that had urged her before, afterwards prompted her to hang herself'

the conjunctive order of the last sentence seems sufficiently explained by the interjectional Witodlice. In prose, therefore, we can confidently say that there is no example of the interception of an unstressed pronoun which is well certified, outside the few forms of it which we have found (62, 63) to be regular.

66. A word must now be said about the order of pronouns among themselves; they often form a syntactical group both in principal and subordinate sentences. The normal precedence is

Subject, Direct object, Indirect object, e.g. agif þu hit me 'give it to me':

Hom. II. 324. 23. Gif we hit forsuwian dorston ne sæde we hit eow 'Had we dared to pass it over in silence we should not have mentioned it to you'.

In these sentences the pronouns are, of course, without stress; any one pronoun, however, may be stressed, in which case it usually takes precedence, e.g.

Hom. I. 76. 6. Ðé we heriað and þanciað (instead of 'we ðe') 'Thée we praise and thank...'
Matt. xvi. 19. ond þé ic sylle heofona rices cægia (instead of 'ic þe') 'and to thée I will give the keys of heaven'.
Hom. I. 598. 8. Ðín me ofhrywð and þinre yrmðe (instead of 'me ðin') 'It is for thée I grieve and for thy misery'.

There can, however, be no such justification for Ða þe him hine ondrædað 'those who fear him', which occurs more than once (e.g. *Blick.* 7. 7); this may be a scribal error for Ða þe hine him ondrædað. It will be convenient here to consider the well-known crux

Beo. 2157   þæt ic his ærest ðe   est gesægde;

It may seem rash to offer an opinion on this much-annotated passage, but it can be said with confidence that *his* must be stressed before *ærest* (63), and it is this stress-pointing word which justifies the separation of *his* from its noun *est*. The literal meaning is therefore '(he bade me) mention to thee íts (i.e. the armour's) presentation first, because it once belonged to King Heorogar'. This gives the sense we expect; for the meaning of 'est', cf. 2165 est geteah 'made a presentation'. The position of *ðe*, outside the pronoun group yet separated from the verb, is difficult to understand; the normal order would be 'þæt ic þe his ærest' metrically a C-type.

67. Yet another syntactical combination is that of finite verb + verbal, of which we shall consider the two forms

(i) copula + participle, e.g. Heo wæs gehaten Livia;
(ii) auxiliary + infinitive, e.g. We sculon weorðian þone halgan.

The verbals in both types were idiomatically end-words, as in Heo wæs L. gehaten, We sculon þone halgan weorðian. Can we

invert the order and say (e.g.) Heo gehaten wæs Livia? We have
already examined sentences with this order when introduced by
þa þær þonne and similar head-words, and have seen that they are
invariably subordinate. Let us look at some different types from
Bede:

148. 24.   Swa gen to dæge Bretta þeaw is.
152. 7.   Se Osric þurh S. Paulines lare gelæred wæs.
296. 13.   Æghwæðer þara þinga swa gefylled wæs.

These are all printed as principal sentences and at first sight the
last two seem beyond doubt; but the Latin shows that they are all
subordinate clauses, Swa meaning 'as', Se Osric 'which Osric'
(*se* being a relative adjective) and þara þinga 'of which things'
(quod ita utrumque) in spite of its internal position which is
evidently a scribal error.

152. 11.   In þas twa mægða Norðhymbra ðeod todæled wæs.
208. 5.   Ðissum tidum þam rice Sigeberht fore wæs.
46.   5.   Ðone man nu to dæg sceawian mæg.

In 46. 5 the Latin (quem videlicet) indicates clearly a relative
clause, in 208. 6 'fore wæs' renders 'praefuit' and should obviously
be printed as one word, while in 152. 11 it is evident from the Latin
(*nam* in has duas provincias, etc.) that a causal conjunction has
been omitted which would make the OE order normal. The two
examples in *ASC*, 642 P Her Oswold cyning ofslægen wæs, 645 P
Her Cenwalh adrifen wæs, are not supported by E, which has 'wæs
ofslagen' and 'wæs adrifen'. There is a somewhat remarkable
instance in

Oros. 56. 14.   Ærþæm þe Romeburg getimbred wære XXgum
wintrum, Læcedemonie and Mesiane him betweonum winnende
wæron.

Now this is a stock opening of a new paragraph in *Orosius*, but the
principal sentence is usually introduced by *wæs þæt* or simply *þæt*,
e.g. (in the preceding paragraph) Ærþæm, etc., wæs þæt Pelopen-
sium ond Atheniensium þeoda...winnende wæron; we must
assume that in 56. 14 *þæt* (with which the syntax becomes normal)
was accidentally omitted, which might easily happen. In

Hom. II. 334. 9.   Ða ðry englas gelicere beorhtnysse scienende
wæron

'Ða' must be a relative adjective (as in *Bede* 152. 7 above) 'which three angels shone with the same brightness'. There is thus no indubitable instance of inversion in a principal sentence, and we conclude that this order is invariably the mark of a subordinate clause. It should be noted that if both verbals, participle and infinitive, are combined in the same clause several varieties of order are possible, all of which occur frequently, viz. ær hit mihte geendod beon, ær hit mihte beon geendod, ær hit geendod beon mihte: only the last of these has conjunctive order, the test of it being the inversion of the finite verb and its verbal, i.e. beon mihte.

68. We now go on to consider whether our rules are valid in verse, and begin with apparent exceptions in *Beowulf* to the rule forbidding interception of an unstressed pronoun. In 40 him on bearme læg..., 726 him of eagum stod..., 816 him on eaxle wearð..., and the like, we have, of course, the normal construction (57) in which the pronoun depends on the noun and not on the verb. Other supposed exceptions are really unsuspected instances of the *he þa* form of sentence, e.g.

1333   Heo þa fæhðe wræc
        þe þu gystran niht Grendel cwealdest
1900   He þæm batwearde bunden golde
        swurd gesealde
2989   He ð[am] frætwum feng

In the last, the original may well have been 'ða' (the MS. is defective), and in 1900 we have only to suppose a 'þa' misread as 'þā'.

69. Next, there are three poetic idioms for each of which one example must suffice since they will be dealt with at length in Chapter IX:

(i)   1138   Ða wæs winter scacen;... fundode wrecca
           gist of geardum;   he to gyrnwræce
           swiðor þohte   þonne to sælade.
(ii)   258   Him se yldesta   ondswarode:
(iii) 2165   he him est geteah
           meara ond maðma.

In (i) a stress on the pronoun, required by the sense, makes the syntax normal. It should be written, however, as one sentence, not three, viz. 'when winter was over and the stranger (at Finn's court) was eager to be gone, hé (Hengest) thought more of vengeance than of sea-faring'; the singular 'wrecca' is generic, i.e. 'all weatherbound men'. In (ii) the pronoun has the position-stress familiar in all English poetry, cf. Milton's 'Him the Ammonite worshipped in Rabba'. In (iii) a stress on either pronoun is meaningless, and the sentence only seems explicable as a co-ordinate clause to 'þam frætwum feower mearas last weardodon' (see 97).

70. We have discussed already derangements of order in the pronoun-group in *Beowulf*, and conclude this survey with the instances of inversion in the combination finite verb + verbal which have not been already dealt with in Chapters II, III:

1239	Bencþelu beredon;	hit geondbræded wearð
	beddum ond bolstrum.	
2692		heals ealne ymbefeng
	biteran banum;	he geblodegod wearð [sawuldriore]

In each passage the order points to the second sentence being a clause, and the right sense is given by the idiomatic and easily omitted *þæt*: 'they cleared the bench-floor so that it was spread with bedding', 'he bit through his neck so that it was all bloody'. In sentences like

636		Ic gefremman sceal
	eorlic ellen	
2275		He gesecean sceal [hord]

ond or another conjunction must have been dropped (see 26 for examples); in 2275 the MS. is defective.

71. Our conclusions in this chapter may be summed up as follows:

(1) Personal pronouns standing in a syntactical relation to the verb are normally not separated from it in a principal sentence.

(2) The unstressed subject-pronoun in an affirmative statement, if the head-word, is immediately followed by the verb, except when the pronoun is further defined by an adjective or noun, e.g. ic sylf, we begen, or is followed by certain kinds of adverb.

(3) The same is true of a governed pronoun when the subject is

not a pronoun, e.g. Him sceamode þæs wordes, Him þa þæs wordes sceamode, but not Him þæs wordes sceamode.

(4) In the pronoun-group the normal order of precedence is *he hine him*, but stress may give priority to a pronoun in any oblique case.

(5) In the syntactical combination finite verb + verbal (is gehaten, mæg secgan) the order is as shown in a normal principal sentence; inversion is always a mark of conjunctive order and therefore of a subordinate or co-ordinate clause.

CHAPTER VII

NEGATIVE WORDS AND SENTENCES

72. The verb in OE was negatived by the particle *ne*, which was always prefixed to it; and in any negative principal sentence the verb thus qualified was normally the head-word, e.g. Ne forseah Crist his geongan cempan 'Christ did not despise his young champions', Næron hie blinde gesceapene 'They were not created blind', Ne mette he ær nan gebun land 'He found no inhabited land before that'. The subject occasionally stands first, if a personal pronoun, e.g. Heo nolde hit hire gemacan secgan. Pronouns in the oblique cases, however, always follow the verb, e.g. Ne þuhte him (but Him þuhte), Nis eow to witenne (but Us is to witenne), etc.; in *Hom.* I. 288. 3 Him ne wiðstent nan ðing 'Hím no object can withstand [as it withstands the sun]', the exception is only apparent since here the pronoun has rhetorical stress. On the other hand, the negative of the substantive verb (nis, næs, etc.) invariably stands first if the subject is any stressed pronoun, e.g. nis þis gecweden, næs þæt seo ærste sið: we have a solitary exception in *Hom.* II. 40. 15 Ðis nis nu alyfed nanum to donne, which might easily be a misreading of Nis ðis. Expletive *þær*, being unstressed, retains its front position even before *næs*, e.g. (in both clauses) *Hom.* I. 176. 7 Ðær næs eac nan geþafung forðam þær næs nan lustfullung 'There was no consent either because there was no pleasure'. When, however, *þær* is stressed and has its full meaning the order is 'næs (nis) þær' as in *Blick.* 25. 25 where there are several antithetical 'þær is' 'nis þær' sentences. In *Hom.* I. 52. 7 Ðær nis Paulus gescynd þurh Stephanes slege, expletive *þær* being meaningless, the sentence should be punctuated as a clause: 'wherein Paul is not shamed by Stephen's slaying [but S. rejoices in the fellowship of Paul]'.

73. A negative principal sentence may be followed by a negative co-ordinate clause introduced by *ne*, which is no longer the negative particle but a conjunction, e.g. He ne cidde ne he ne hrymde 'he chided not nor did he cry'; it will be observed that the

negative particle may be retained before the verb in the co-ordinate clause. The regular order in such a clause is conjunctive, as will be seen from the following examples:

Hom. I. 80. 34. Næs he æðelboren ne him naht to þam cynecynne ne gebyrode 'He was not noble-born nor was he connected in any way with the royal family'.

I. 572. 3. Ne geseah ic næfre ða burh ne ic ðone seað nat 'I never saw the city nor do I know the pit'.

Gen. xix. 17. Ne beseoh þu under bæc ne þu ne ætstande 'Look not behind nor do thou tarry'.

The examples show also that, even when the subject does not change, the pronoun, contrary to ModE idiom, is usually repeated in the co-ordinate clause; it may indeed be repeated in more than one clause, e.g.

Hom. I. 320. 14. He ne hrymde ne he biterwyrde næs ne he sace ne astyrede 'He cried not nor bore malice nor stirred up strife'.

The pronoun, however, is sometimes omitted as in *Hom.* II. 40. 16 He ne wiðerode ongean ne ne feaht, and then the conjunction and the negative particle in the co-ordinate clause may fall together. This is not uncommon in the OE translation of the Bible, e.g. þa fleogendan fugelas ðe ne sawað ne ne ripað 'the birds of the air which sow not nor reap', ne slæpð ne ne hnappað seðe hylt Israhel 'He that watches over Israel sleeps not nor slumbers'. Occasionally the negative particle is dropped, and then the co-ordinate clause may be indistinguishable from a principal sentence, e.g.

Hom. II. 46. 16. Ne deð seo culfre na swa ne leofað heo be nanum deaðe 'The dove does not do so nor does she live by any death',

where the second *ne* is of course the conjunction.

74. The converse, however, is never true, and we can lay down the general rule that *ne* never introduces a principal sentence unless it is followed immediately by the verb. Yet principal sentences of the form 'Ne heo andswarode' are not uncommon in our texts as printed, e.g. *Hom.* I. 278. 2 Ne worhte se Fæder nan ðing ne ne wyrcð butan ðam Suna oððe þam Halgan Gaste. Ne heora nan ne wyrcð nan ðing butan oðrum (so T.): the sentences are co-ordinate and mean 'The Father has created and creates nothing without the Son and the Holy Ghost, [nor] does any of them do

anything without the others'. Here no great harm is done by the separation of the co-ordinate clause, but there are contexts where it is very damaging to the sense, e.g.

Hom. II. 6. 29. Gif he come on ðære Godcundnysse buton menn-iscnysse þonne ne mihte ure tyddernys aberan his mihte. Ne seo Godcundnys ne mihte nan ðing þrowian forðan þe heo is unðrowi-gendlic (So T.).

Here Thorpe's rendering of the second sentence 'The Godhead could suffer nothing because it is impassible' quite misses the point. Ælfric is explaining why Christ came to earth as a man; had He come in His Godhead 'in that case our weakness could not have endured his power nor would Godhead either have been able to suffer since Godhead is impassible'. It is important that *both* consequences, hypothetical not actual, of a different scheme of salvation should be stated together. Again, in

Hom. II. 94 ft. Ne heora nan gerefscipe oððe mangunge ne drife forðan ðe hi sind gecorene to Godes teolungum (So T.).

Thorpe's rendering 'Let none of them undertake any reeveship or mongering' misrepresents the prohibition as Ælfric's own. The sentence, however, is a continuation of the monastic rule which Ælfric is expounding and depends on *þæt* five lines before; there is a double prohibition in the rule, 'that no priest have any female in his dwelling, etc., *and* that he do not undertake any public office or trade'. Again, in

Hom. I. 6. 13. Ne sende se deofol ða fyr of heofonum þeah ðe hit ufan come.... Ne eac se wælhreowa Antecrist næfð ða mihte þæt he heofonlic fyr asendan mæge (So T.).

Ælfric has been comparing the work of Antichrist with that of the devil in the tempting of Job, and his comparison is summed up in these two sentences: 'Just as on that occasion the devil did not send fire from heaven though it came from above, so also will the cruel Antichrist not have the power to send down heavenly fire.' There is not a single instance in any text translated from Latin which justifies Thorpe's construction.

75. In Modern English there is a use of 'nor' (=not either) which is foreign to OE idiom, as in the sentence (which may even begin a new paragraph) 'Nor was the King wholly to blame'. This

'nor', since it does not introduce a co-ordinate clause, can never
be rendered by the OE conjunction *ne* but must be broken up into
ne...eac, where *ne* is the negative particle and must, of course, be
attached to the verb; one instance of the idiom will suffice, *Hom.* I.
40 ft. Nis eac Cristes godcundnys gerunnen to ðære menniscnysse
'Nor is Christ's divine nature confused with the human'. *Hom.* I.
176. 7, I. 6. 13 cited above (72, 74) are other instances. There are
some contexts in which the co-ordinate form of the negative sentence appears, somewhat strangely, after a question, e.g. *Bede*
348. 2 Þa ondswarodon heo ond cwædon Hwylc þearf is ðe husles?
Ne þinre forðfore swa neah is..., where the translation has 'What
need have you of the Eucharist? You are not so near your death'.
As it appears elsewhere, this might be taken to be a veritable OE
idiom; inspection of the original, however, shows that in all cases
the second sentence is an attempt to render a Latin clause beginning *neque enim* (=since not) and should therefore be included
within the interrogation. And the same explanation no doubt
holds for examples in non-Latin texts, e.g.

Blick. 21 ft. Hwylc bið he þonne buton swylce stan? Ne he hine na
ne onstyreð syððan seo sawl him of bið 'What will he then be but,
as it were, a stone, unable to move when once the soul is out of him?'

76. There are, however, other instances which are pure Latinisms
and cannot be corrected by repunctuation. The translator of *Bede*
renders the idiomatic Latin Nec mora, at the beginning of a sentence, by 'Ne heo þa ne ælde' or the like. Ne quidem, again, is a
frequent stumbling-block to him, and 'ne tum quidem' 'ne sic
quidem' 'ne adhuc quidem' all alike appear as Ne þa gena, e.g.
286. 19 Ond ne þa gena þeah heo þus spræce ænig onswarade 'And
not even when she spoke thus did anyone answer'. In *Matt.* xxi. 27
we have a Latin idiom of another kind: Ne ic eow ne secge 'neither
do Í say to you' where *V.* has Nec ego dico vobis; and yet another
in *Num.* xxiii. 25 Ne þu hine wirige ne þu hine bletsa 'Neither
curse them nor bless them' (*V.* Nec maledicas eos nec benedicas),
which makes the syntax in *both* OE sentences that of a co-ordinate
clause (see 59). And *Matt.* vi. 29 ne Salomon in allum his wuldre
(Rushworth) is an attempt to render *nec* in yet another sense, viz.
'not even'. All these are specimens of crib-English which cannot
be matched in any piece of native prose.

77. The negative co-ordinate clause after an affirmative sentence is normally introduced, as in Modern English, by *ond ne*, where of course *ne* is the negative particle, e.g.

Hom. II. 68. 15. Doð swa swa hi tæcað ond ne do ge swa swa hi doð 'Do as they teach and not as they do'.

Gen. iv. 5. Ða beseah he to Abele and ne beseah to Caine 'Then he looked upon Abel and looked not upon Cain'

though a co-ordinate clause with the conjunction *ne* is also found, e.g.

Hom. I. 580. 16. God sceawað þæs mannes heortan. Ne he ne telð hu micele speda we aspendon (So T.) 'God looks at a man's heart and does not reckon how great riches we spend'.

Normally, however, a *ne*-clause after an affirmative sentence has a particular shade of meaning which may be rendered by an adverbial phrase introduced by 'without', e.g. Ic þa hine lange beseah ne ic hine oncnawan mihte 'I then looked at him for a long time without being able to recognize him'; and so in

Bede 160. 16. Ferde he geond eall ne he on horses hricge cuman wolde 'He went everywhere without ever mounting horse'.

LS I. 16. 112. Seo sawul bið betere ne heo ne undergæð lichamlice mycelnis 'The soul is better, though without bodily increase'.

Hom. II. 124. 10. Gehwilce ænlipige sind mid færlicum slihte aweste. Ne seo adl ðam deaðe ne forestæpð (So T.) 'Each one individually is destroyed by sudden stroke without any preceding illness'.

And so, naturally, with *hwæðre* in the clause:

Hom. II. 18. 10. Gif we willað areccan ealle ða gewitnyssa, þonne gæð swiðe micel hwil to; ne þeahhwæðere we ne magon hi ealle gereccan (So T.) 'If we seek to recount all the testimonies it will take a very long time without our being able even then to go through them all'.

Bede 212. 14. Ða fliton him on þa wergan gastas; ne heo hwæðre owiht in þon fromedon (So M.) 'The accursed spirits fought against him without however achieving anything'.

That the clause should never be separated, as in these examples, from the principal sentence is shown by the fact that the construction occurs within the subordinate clause, e.g.:

Bede 98. 21. Ða heo ða hæfdon longe spræce ne heo Agustines larum ne benum geþafian woldon... 'When they had had a long discussion without consenting to accept Augustine's teachings or listen to his prayers...'.

78. A few instances may be added from verse:

Beo. 862   monig oft gecwæð
              þætte...oðer nænig
              under swegles begong   selra nære.
              Ne hie huru winedrihten wiht ne logon.

i.e. 'though they belittled not their own dear lord'.

Beo. 2277   þær he hæðen gold
              warað wintrum frod;   ne bið him wihte ðy sel
              'where he watches heathen gold yet has no profit from it'.
  1536 þonne he æt guðe   gegan þenceð
              longsumne lof,   na ymb his lif cearað
              'when he is minded to win fame without recking of life'.
  1735 Wunað he on wiste;   no hine wiht dweleð
              adl ne yldo
              'He lives in plenty without the affliction of sickness or old
              age'.

In all these there should be nothing more than a comma after the
first sentence; it may be suspected that *na* (no) is a scribal error
for *ne* in the last two. In

Beo. 506   Eart þu se Beowulf   seþe wið Brecan wunne
              ðær git for wlence   wada cunnedon...?
                        ...Ne inc ænig mon
              ne leof ne lað   belean mihte

the negative clause should be placed inside the question 'when ye
essayed the floods in your pride and no man, friend or foe, could
deny you?' Instances of the more usual co-ordinate clause (74) are

Beo. 739 Ne þæt se aglæca   yldan þohte
      1071 Ne huru Hildeburh   herian þorfte
      2922 Ne ic to Sweoðeode   sibbe oððe treowe | ne wene

These also should not be separated from the preceding sentence.

79. We shall now turn to some of the Disjunctive negatives,
beginning with *no*. This is used to negate any part of speech other
than a finite verb, e.g. na Romane ac elþeodig 'not a Roman but a
foreigner', na elles 'not otherwise',

  Hom. I. 352. 18. He wæs Godes bydel ond na God 'He was God's
messenger and not God'.
  II. 34. 10. na ongean feohtende ac sweltende 'not fighting against
it but dying'.

I. 400. 12. Godes miht þe gehælde na ic 'God's power has healed thee, not I'.

I. 390 ft. na þæt he nolde for Cristes geleafan deað þrowian 'not that he would not suffer death for Christ'.

It cannot in good prose be used to negate the verb except in conjunction with the negative particle, and rare instances like

Hom. I. 550 ft. na beoð þa eadige þe for hynðum heofiað 'they are not blessed who mourn for misfortune'.

ASC 1001 A. þe we genemnan na cunnon 'which we cannot name'

must be scribal errors; in fact, the same paragraph in *ASC* has 'þe we genemnan ne cunnan' a few lines before.

80. The pleonastic negative with a verb occurs in all prose texts, and the more frequently the later the writing; it is, perhaps, most common in the WS *Gospels* especially in the phrase Nis na (næs na). In Ælfric's *Homilies* it is found twenty-four times in the first 100 pages, twelve of the instances being Nis na (næs na) while in the rest the verb is stressed: in some of the latter the *na* perhaps negates a specific word, e.g.

I. 20. 4. we forluron þa gesælðe ure sawle ac we ne forluron na þa undeadlicnysse 'we lost the happiness of our soul but not its immortality'.

I. 138. 7. Ne sohte Crist na ða modigan [ac ða eaðmodan] 'Christ sought not the proud [but the humble]'.

In the *Chronicle* there is only one instance 894 A þa ne mihte seo fird hie na hindan offaran, and in *Beowulf* the solitary example is in the corrupt line

1508   swa he ne mihte no he þæm modig wæs

A much rarer order is when the *no* precedes the negative verb, e.g.

Matt. xviii. 13. þa nigon ond hundnigontig þe na ne losedon 'the ninety and nine that did not stray'.

Hom. I. 298. 24. ge þær hi bodedon ge þær þær hi na ne becomon 'both where they preached and where they did not come'.

CP 198. 13. swa hit him no ne derige 'in such a way as not to injure him'.

In all these examples, it will be observed, the verb has the conjunctive *ne*; without the conjunctive negative *no* (*na*) occurs, though rarely, in verse, e.g.

Beo. 2585   guðbill geswac...swa hyt no sceolde,

but in prose only in a few glosses from the Vespasian *Hymns* or the Rushworth *Gospels*, which can scarcely be held to certify general usage. When it occurs in verse, the negative is usually next before the verb, and this order, in our poetic tradition, has survived into modern times; the examples in NED come down as late as Byron 'To make a marvel that it not decay', and prove that in Modern as in Old English the negative was, in this position, stressed.

81. A few words must now be said about another use of *no* which is almost entirely confined to poetry. Here it is never used as it is in prose (Godes bydel no God) to negate one of two alternatives; this sense is always expressed by *nales*, e.g. fea nales monge 'few not many'. Its characteristic use in poetry is before a stressed pronoun, as in *Beo.* 1355 no hie fæder cunnon. This means, however, not 'it is not they that know his father' but simply 'théy know not his father', i.e. it is the poetic form of 'hie ne cunnon fæder' when *hie* is stressed. Similarly, 1002 No þæt yðe byð, means no more than Nis þæt yðe 'thát is not easy' and not 'it is not that which is easy (but something else)'. Some other instances may be cited:

Beo. 445   Na þu minne þearft
              hafalan hydan
              'Thóu wilt not need to hide my head'.

       581   No ic wiht fram þe
              swylcra searoniða secgan hyrde
              'Í never heard such exploits told of thee'.

      2354   No þæt læsest wæs
              hondgemota, þær mon Hygelac sloh
              'Thát was not the least of hand-to-hand fights when they
              slew Hygelac'.

       541   No he wiht fram me
              flodyðum feor fleotan meahte...
                            no ic fram him wolde.

Here the verbs as well as the subjects are contrasted 'hé could not swim far away from me, nor would Í from hím', and the second *no* (in a co-ordinate clause) may be a scribal error for *ne*. Since 'no þæt yðe bið' has obviously the same metrical pattern as 2415 næs þæt yðe ceap (Sievers' type E with an anacrustic syllable), it appears certain that *no* in all these contexts was unstressed. The stressed form of the disjunctive negative in verse was *nales*, to which we now turn.

82. That *nales* (*nealles, nallas*, etc.) was stressed is clear from many instances where otherwise we have a short line, e.g. *Beo.* 43, 562, 2145, 2221; it is used in verse like *no* in prose, i.e. to negate a particular word, especially one of two alternatives, e.g. *Beo.* 3089 nealles swæslice 'in no pleasant way', 3019 oft nalles æne 'not once but often',

338   Wen ic þæt ge for wlenco nalles for wræcsiðum
               . . . Hroðgar sohton
      'Methinks ye have sought H. in pride of spirit, not as exiled men'

It is also used, however, quite frequently, as a head-word to negate a sentence, e.g.

2873   Nealles folccyning fyrdgesteallum
      gylpan þorfte
      'By no means could our King boast of his comrades-in-arms'.

The short form is *næs*, and this, for metrical reasons, should obviously be the reading in

1442   nalles for ealdre mearn

Nales is occasionally found in prose, but only in the first sense above mentioned, e.g. nales þæt an þæt (=no þæt an þæt 'not only') more than once in *Bede, Oros.* 102. 5 nales (L. na) swa hit gewuna is 'not as is usual'; a remarkable instance is

Lev. i. 17. Abred of þa fiðeru næs ne cerfe 'Thou shalt pull off the wings but not cut them'

since here it negates a verb.

83. In *Beowulf* there is another negative phrase, viz. *no þy ær* 'none the more'. It has the force of the adversative conjunction 'yet not', e.g.

Beo. 1502   guðrinc gefeng
      atolan clommum;   no þy ær in gescod . . .
      '[she] seized him with her dread claws, yet could not harm . . .' (the semicolon should be a comma);

and it is, therefore, sometimes correlated with *þeah*, e.g.

Beo. 2160　no ðy ær suna sinum syllan wolde
　　　　...þeah he him hold wære
　　　'yet would not give the arms to his own son for all that he
　　　was friendly to him'.

84. Finally, mention must be made of *noðer*. This negative is not a conjunction but a pronominal, like its opposite *ægðer*, and both of them are properly followed by a pair of co-ordinating conjunctions, e.g. *ægðer ge god ge yfel* 'both good and evil', *noðer ne god ne yfel* 'neither good nor evil'. There is, therefore, something wrong wherever *noðer* appears itself to be a conjunction; e.g. in

Beo. 2124　Þær wæs Æschere... feorh uðgenge.
　　　　Noðer hy hine ne moston,　　syððan mergen cwom,
　　　　bronde forbærnan　　ne on bæl hladan

no þy ær gives exactly the right sense, and the extreme rarity of this phrase (if it occurs at all) outside *Beowulf* would explain the scribal error: 'there was A. reft of life, yet might they not, when morning came, burn him with fire nor lay him on the pyre.' The only alternative to making *noðer* = 'nor' (as given by the glossaries) is to regard the two infinitives 'bronde forbærnan' and 'ne on bæl hladan' as bracketed by 'noðer' in the usual way ('neither burn him nor lay him on the pyre'): this, however, would be no less a solecism, since the two clauses are synonymous and not, as they should be, mutually exclusive.

CHAPTER VIII

POETIC IDIOMS: (i) THE ASYNDETIC
CO-ORDINATE CLAUSE

85. We shall deal in this and the next two chapters with some idioms which are confined to OE poetry, and begin with one which is wrongly called parataxis but is really asyndetic co-ordination. The co-ordinate clause without conjunction is often correctly shown in modern editions when it is co-ordinate to a principal sentence as in

Beo. 7   he þæs frofre gebad,
         weox under wolcnum, weorðmyndum þah,

though there are many instances in which it is not, e.g.

    358   Hwearf þa hrædlice þær Hroðgar gesæt;...
             eode ellenrof þæt he for eaxlum gestod

where the stop should be a comma: 'he turned quickly to where H. sat [and] went and stood, gallant man, at his shoulder'. It is, however, quite the exception to find such a clause recognised when co-ordinate to a dependent sentence. To familiarise the reader with the type let us take a preliminary survey of six examples from *Beowulf*:

    89   þær wæs hearpan sweg,
         swutol sang scopes;   sægde seþe cuþe
         frumsceaft fira   feorran reccan...
    891   þæt hit on wealle stod,
         dryhtlic iren;   draca morðre sweallt.
    1256   þætte wrecend þa gyt
         lifde æfter laþum...;   Grendles modor,
         ides, aglæcwif, yrmþe gemunde

The co-ordination is obvious, and the second sentence should not be separated from the first by more than a comma: 'when there rose the minstrel's clear song, [and] one that knew the story of man's creation told...', 'so that it (the sword) stood fast in the wall [and] the dragon died violently', 'it was seen that an avenger survived the loathly one [and] that Grendel's mother remembered her affliction '. In all these each of the two sentences has its proper subject, but in the following, where the subject is the same, it is idiomatically unexpressed in the second:

1318   þæt he þone wisan   wordum nægde
        frean Ingwina;   frægn gif him wære
        æfter neodlaðum   niht getæse

'to greet the wise prince of the Ingwines [and] ask him if he had had a peaceful night'.

2391   se ðæs leodhryres   lean gemunde
        uferan dogrum;   Eadgilse wearð
        feasceaftum freond

'who in after days avenged his lord's downfall [and] befriended the hapless Eadgils'. The second clause is frequently a negative paraphrase of the first, as in

2918   þæt se byrnwiga   bugan sceolde,
        feoll on feðan;   nalles frætwe geaf
        ealdor duguðe

'that the warrior bowed to his death [and] nowise gave treasure, as a leader should, to his fighting men'; replace the semicolons in all the above passages by commas.

86. The form we have just illustrated is the regular one in OE poetry for the co-ordinate clause and we can enunciate two rules about it:

(i) that the co-ordinate clause to a principal or subordinate sentence is normally asyndetic;

(ii) that, if the subject in the two sentences is the same, it is expressed in the first only and not in the second.

87. In the light of these two rules let us look at some further examples from *Beowulf*, in which the traditional text misses co-ordination to a principal sentence:

1310   Hraðe wæs to bure   Beowulf fetod,
        sigoreadig secg;   samod ærdæge | eode
1810   cwæð he þone guðwine godne tealde
        wigcræftigne;   nales wordum log
        meces ecge

In each of these the second sentence is a positive or negative paraphrase of the first; 'Beowulf was quickly fetched [and] at daybreak went to the bower', 'said that he accounted the war-friend a good one [nor] belied the weapon's edge'. Again, the second sentence may complete the sense of the first, as in

```
1233    druncon win weras:      wyrd ne cuþon
2703                  wællseaxe gebræd
        biter ond beaduscearp   þæt he on byrnan wæg;
        forwrat, Wedra helm,    wyrm on middan
```

'the men drank wine [and] knew not of fate', 'he drew his short-sword, bitter and battle-sharp, [and] slit the worm at the waist'; or it may amplify the first by adding a command or request, e.g.

```
1043    Ond ða Beowulfe...onweald geteah
        wicga ond wæpna;      het hine wel brucan
```

'and then gave B. possession of horses and weapons, bidding him have good joy of them'.

88. The reader may think that in principal sentences like these no great harm is done by the separation of the clauses; let us therefore take some examples in which the co-ordinated sentences are both dependent on a third in order to see how the accepted punctuation disintegrates the syntactical structure. Clauses introduced by a variety of conjunctions have been selected by way of illustration:

```
415           me þæt gelærdon...þæt ic þe sohte,
        forþan hie mægenes cræft      minne cuþon;
        selfe ofersawon      ða ic of searwum cwom
```

Here 'ofersawon' is clearly co-ordinate to 'cuþon', not to 'gelærdon', and the two verbs have not only a common subject but a common object as well; 'since they well knew the power of my strength [and] had seen it themselves when I came from straits of battle'.

```
622              sæl alamp
        þæt hio Beowulfe...medoful ætbær;
        grette Geata leod,   Gode þancode
```

Here 'grette' and 'þancode' complete the action of 'ætbær' and should obviously not be separated from it: 'time came when she brought the mead-cup to Beowulf, greeted the Geatish lord, and thanked God...'. Somewhat similar are

881
      swa hie a wæron
 æt niða gehwam nydgesteallan;
 hæfdon ealfela eotena cynnes
 sweordum gesæged

'since they had ever been comrades in arms [and] had slain with their swords many of the ettin race'.

2280
      oð ðæt hyne an abealch
 man on mode; mandryhtne bær
 fæted wæge

'till one made him angry at heart, [when] he took to his lord the cup of gold'; in both these the second clause particularises the action of the preceding verb. We have yet another shade of meaning in

2369 Þær him Hygd gebead hord ond rice,
   beagas ond bregostol: bearne ne truwode
   þæt he...healdan cuðe

where 'truwode' supplies the motive for 'gebead': 'when Hygd offered him the kingdom, not trusting her son's power to hold it.' In each of these passages, as in the last group considered, the second sentence is necessary to complete in some way the sense of the first one; does not the reader feel that the colons and semi-colons ruin the syntactical structure? The effect is exactly the same as if we placed a colon after 'equall'd' in Milton's

     farthest from him is best
 Whom reason hath equall'd, force hath made supreme
 Above his equals,

or a colon after 'eternity' in his

    since God is light
 And never but in unapproachèd light
 Dwelt from eternity, dwelt then in thee.

It will be observed that in the last line such a punctuation would leave us a subjectless verb, as in the *Beowulf* examples; this raises another grammatical problem with which we must deal presently.

89. Let us now examine some other instances from *Beowulf* in which failure to co-ordinate not merely obscures the sense intended but positively suggests a wrong one:

322   hringiren scir
        song in searwum   þa hie to sele furþum
        in hyra gryregeatwum   gangan cwomon.
        Setton sæmeþe   side scyldas....

There are two faults here: the *þa*-clause is attached to the wrong sentence, and it is severed from the right one. What is the point of saying that the ringed iron sang as soon as they reached the hall? Place the full-stop after 'searwum'; the poet has told us how the byrnies gleamed and the iron sang as they marched, and he continues 'as soon as they had reached the hall [and], sea-wearied men, had set their broad shields against the wall, [they bowed to the bench]'. This is the sense we expect; no sense can be got out of the text as it stands.

1465   Huru ne gemunde   mago Ecglafes
        þæt he ær gespræc...þa he þæs wæpnes onlah
        selran sweordfrecan;   selfa ne dorste
        under yða gewin   aldre geneþan

With this punctuation it is certain that in any period of English the reader would take the last sentence as co-ordinate to 'ne gemunde' and explaining it, and would, therefore, be misled into supposing that what Unferth had said in his cups was that he would venture his life beneath the waters, and that he was now too cowardly to do so. The sense is clear if we make the last sentence co-ordinate to 'onlah', i.e. 'when he lent his weapon to a better swordsman [and] did not dare himself to hazard his life'. We have exactly the same type of sentence in

3066   Swa wæs Biowulfe,   þa he biorges weard
        sohte searoniða;   seolfa ne cuþe
        þurh hwæt his worulde gedal   weorðan sceolde

where 'ne cuþe', as printed, must be construed as co-ordinate to 'wæs', and we mistakenly suppose that Beowulf's misfortune was that he did not know the manner of his own death; take 'ne cuþe' into the *þa*-clause and we have 'It befell Beowulf, when he attacked the dragon little knowing how he should die, [according to the ancient curse]'. It may be observed that in both the above passages 'selfa', being adjectival, cannot itself stand as a subject but needs the support of 'he' in the clause before.

2158 cwæð þæt hyt hæfde Hiorogar cyning;
    no þy ær suna sinum syllan wolde

The punctuation should show that the second line, like the first, is part of Hroðgar's statement 'that Herogar had it long, yet would not give it to his son'; the text as it stands makes it Beowulf's. And so frequently elsewhere, e.g.

94 gesette sigehreðig sunnan ond monan...
    ond gefrætwade foldan sceatas
    leomum ond leafum; lif eac gesceop

where 'gesceop', like 'gesette', must depend on 'cwæð þæt'; to make 'gesceop' a separate sentence, as the traditional text does, is to assign it to the writer of the poem instead of the 'scop'.

2613 Weohstan...his magum ætbær
    ealdsweord etonisc, þæt him Onela forgeaf,
    his gædelinges guðgewædu,
    fyrdsearo fuslic; no ymb ða fæhðe spræc

With this punctuation anyone would suppose that it was Weohstan who said nothing about the feud, and so some editors take it: the sense we expect however is 'which Onela gave him without saying a word about the feud' (in which W. had killed Onela's kinsman), and for this we need a comma instead of a semicolon after 'fuslic'. Weohstan would be the last man to mention the feud.

90. The usually accepted construction in all the passages we have been considering rests on the twofold assumption of an anomalous kind of principal sentence and of a subjectless verb in it, and it is time to deal with the latter problem. Did OE poetic idiom really allow the omission of the subject-pronoun in a principal sentence? There are at least a hundred subjectless principal sentences in the traditional text of *Beowulf*, but it is surely a significant fact that the great majority admit of being taken as co-ordinate clauses, in which as we have seen the omission of the subject, if *the same* as in the preceding sentence, is the regular idiom. Let us now take a glance at the small residue. In some of

them a slight emendation which makes the syntax normal is
accepted by one or more editors, e.g.

1903	gewat him on nacan
2547	ne meahte horde neah
	deop gedygan for dracan lege.
2880	Symle wæs þy sæmra þonne ic sweorde drep
	ferhðgeniðlan;
1291	helm ne gemunde...þa hine se broga angeat
3082	lete hyne licgean þær he longe wæs;
	heold on heahgesceap.

where 'naca' 'deor' 'ferhðgeniðla' 'þe hine' 'healdon' (=healdan)
are convincing; similarly in

470	siððan þa fæhðe feo þingode
2904	sweorde ne meahte
	wunde gewyrcean
2959	freoðowong þone forð ofereodon

personification of the noun-subject is so idiomatic in poetry (e.g.
2488 hond gemunde fæhðo, 2673 byrne ne mihte geoce gefremman)
that 'feoh' 'sweord' may well be the right readings in the first two
and 'segn Higlaces' (l. 2958) the subject in the last.   In

145	Swa rixode...ana wið eallum
179	helle gemundon
	in modsefan, metod hie ne cuðon
402	Snyredon ætsomne þa secg wisode
	under Heorotes hrof:

the poet's usage elsewhere suggests the pronoun 'an' instead of the
adjective 'ana' in 145, cf. 2268 swa mænde an æfter eallum, and
makes it certain that in 179 'hie' has got displaced since it is
required in the first sentence and is otiose in the co-ordinate clause;
in 402, as we have been told in the line before that 'some remained
outside to watch the weapons' and these cannot also have gone
inside, read 'þā' (=þam) for 'þa': 'those whom the hero took with
him hastened to go under Hart's roof.' The emendations in all
these passages require the change of no more than a single letter,
and they are palaeographically probable, for all the scribal errors
assumed (the insertion or omission of final n or m and of the case-
endings -a or -e, the confusion of þa þe þā with each other, wrong
division of words) are of a kind which the scribe has by general

admission made in other places. In any case, such passages can hardly support the general assumption of an omitted subject.

91. Our conclusions about the subjectless verb in *Beowulf* are that in five out of every six instances the supposed principal sentence in which it occurs is really a co-ordinate clause, in which the omission of the subject, if unchanged, has in all periods of English been idiomatic; and that the remaining instances of omission in undoubted principal sentences (about one in every 200 lines) may easily be due to scribal error. We are, of course, not reckoning principal sentences of the 'Com *þa*' type, numbering in *Beowulf* about ninety, in which the verb is the head-word; we have seen (15) that in these omission is the rule even in prose and that the unexpressed subject is to be understood from the sentence before. In verse we also find a verb without subject before enclitic *þonne*, e.g.

Beo. 2460   Gewiteð þonne on sealman

or even before enclitic *swa*, e.g.

Beo. 2057   Manað swa ond myndgað   mæla gehwylce

It is noteworthy that in some OE poems, e.g. *Judith*, there are no examples at all of an omitted subject in principal sentences except in these of the 'Com ða' type.

CHAPTER IX

POETIC IDIOMS: (ii) PRINCIPAL SENTENCES WITH CONJUNCTIVE ORDER

92. Conjunctive order in a principal sentence, with the characteristic interception of the personal pronoun, is comparatively rare in prose; most examples (62 *sqq.*) occur in sentences of the *he þa* form where it is idiomatic. In verse the order is frequent, and the conditions under which it occurs, other than those common to prose and verse, may be classified as follows:

(i) After certain adverbs as head-words. The order is not surprising after connectives like *swylce, þa gyt*, or even after quasi-connectives like *sona, swa, forðam, þy*. We find it also, however, after some adverbs of time, e.g. *nu, oft, symle*, after the negatives *nalas, næfre, no þy ær, no* (he), and after the exclamatory *hwæt*. Examples (all from *Beowulf*) are:

293	Swylce ic maguþegnas mine hate
1866	Ða git him eorla hleo inne gesealde | maþmas
1794	Sona him seleþegn...forð wisade
559	Swa mec gelome laðgeteonan | þreatedon
679	Forþan ic hine sweorde swebban nelle
951	Ful oft ic for læssan lean teohhode
1818	Nu we sæliðend secgan wyllað
43	Nalæs hi hine læssan lacum teodan
655	Næfre ic ænegum ær alyfde
2466	no þy ær he þone heaðorinc hatian ne mihte
2248	Hwæt, hit ær on ðe
	gode begeaton.

We have seen that this order is never found after the adverbs *þa þær þonne*; all supposed instances are really subordinate adverbial clauses, and for apparent exceptions to this rule like *Beo.* 2446 þonne he gyd wrece... there is (27) a good reason.

93. Conjunctive order is the rule (ii) after a pronoun-subject bearing rhetorical stress, e.g.

Beo. 318   íc to sæ wille

(by contrast to 'eowic' in the line before).

2620   Hé frætwe geheold fela missera

(by contrast to 'byre' in the next line) and so frequently. In prose, with rare exceptions, this idiom is found only (63) when the pronoun precedes a superlative like *ærest*, and in such a context it is not uncommon in verse also, e.g.

Beo. 2077   hé fyrmest læg
Cæd. 5.   Hé ærist scop   ælda barnum | heben

94. So also (iii) we have conjunctive order after a pronoun in an oblique case with position stress, e.g.

Beo. 232   hine fyrwyt bræc
    258   Him se yldesta ondswarode
    477   hie wyrd forsweop
   1841   Ðe þa wordcwydas   wittig drihten | sende
   1853   Me þin modsefa
          licað leng swa sel

The stress here is purely conventional (69) and is due (as in all periods of English) to the poetic inversion, for if we write the natural order Se yldesta him andswarode 'the leader answered him' there is no emphasis on the pronoun. Sievers ignores the stress in all these examples, although it is certified by lines like

Beo. 2101   Me þone wælræs   wine Scildunga | leanode
Rid. ix. 9.   Mec seo friðemæg   fedde siþþan

which without it are a stress short.

95. Lastly, we have (iv) a particular variety of (iii). In all the examples just cited the subject is a noun; whenever it is a pronoun, it precedes the stressed pronoun and is proclitic to it. This is proved quite conclusively by lines like

Beo. 426 |ðing wið þyrse.] Ic þe nuða
           biddan wille
   1180   [metodsceaft seon.] Ic minne can
           glædne Hroðulf

where the alliterating words 'þe' and 'minne' must needs be stressed: other examples are

1490   ic me mid Hruntinge
        dom gewyrce
1829   ic þe þusenda   þegna bringe

96. A few words may be said in conclusion on the differences of order in prose and verse in the sentence-forms illustrated above. We find something like (i) in prose, but with one marked difference, viz. the position of the adverb; we saw (62) that the prose order is He symle on his legere Gode ðancode, whereas the order in verse (92) would be Symle he...Gode ðancode (cf. *Beo.* 2497 symle ic him on feðan beforan wolde); the sentence-order in both is, however, conjunctive. With the one exception mentioned in 93 examples of (ii) and (iii) do not normally occur in prose. In (iv) prose and verse differ entirely. A stress on one of two or more pronouns in prose merely alters (66) its place in the pronoun-group without further affecting the sentence-order, e.g. Mé he clypað nu to his rice; the order in verse, however, would be completely conjunctive, i.e. 'he mé nu to his rice clypað' (for examples see 95).

CHAPTER X

POETIC IDIOMS: (iii) DUBIOUS FORMS OF PRINCIPAL SENTENCE

97. In the traditional text of *Beowulf* there are a number of principal sentences superficially like those discussed in the last chapter but which differ from them in two ways, first because there is nothing to suggest a stress on the pronouns and, secondly, because the context does not tolerate a self-contained principal sentence. We begin by considering some instances in which sense points to a co-ordinate clause:

1434   þæt him on aldre stod
herestræl hearda: he on holme wæs
sundes þe sænra
'so that the war-shaft stood in his heart [and] he was the slower in swimming'.

2059   þæt se fæmnan þegn...blodfag swefeð
ealdres scyldig;   him se oðer þonan
losað lifigende
'that the bride's thane sleeps in his blood [and] his slayer escapes with his life'.

2163   Hyrde ic þæt þam frætwum feower mearas
last weardodon...;   he him est geteah
meara ond maðma
'I heard that four horses followed the trappings [and that] he gave him possession of horses and treasure'.

471   sende ic Wylfingum   ofer wæteres hrycg
ealde madmas;   he me aþas swor
'I sent ancient treasure to the Wulfings [and] he swore me oaths (i.e. became my liegeman)'.

The reader will observe that usually in such examples the interception of the pronoun, whether in the nominative or an oblique case, is due to a change of subject and that the second sentence in each passage would be normal if preceded by the conjunction *ond*. Is it possible, we ask ourselves, even in verse, to retain in asyndeton the conjunctive order which is regular only after the conjunction?

98. In order to answer this question we must enquire how the poet uses the conjunction *ond*. It is noteworthy that, whereas it stands almost invariably between pairs of words (e.g. isig ond utfus), it is the exception to find it connecting sentences or clauses; there are only some seventy instances in the whole poem and in more than half of these the use of the conjunction seems specially designed to avoid the word-order we are now considering, e.g.

653	[Gegrette þa...]	ond him hæl abead
1236		[Syþþan æfen cwom]
	ond him Hroðgar gewat	
1834		[þæt ic þe wel herige]
	ond þe to geoce	garholt bere
2138	[holm heolfre weoll]	ond ic heafde becearf
2640	[onmunde usic mærða]	ond me þas maðmas geaf

The general likeness of these sentences to those cited above is striking and suggests rather strongly the insertion of *ond* in the relatively few similar contexts in which it is lacking. The occasional overlooking by a scribe of a small mark like the *ond*-sigil is a possibility that needs no demonstration, and by mere luck we have positive evidence on the point in the four short poems in the *Chronicle* under the years 937, 942, 973, 975. Taken together, these only number 143 lines; yet there are no fewer than nine places in which one MS. at least differs from the rest in the insertion or omission of the conjunction *ond*.

99. Let us carry the argument a step farther. There are in *Beowulf* a number of asyndetic co-ordinate clauses containing an unstressed pronoun but in which the poet avoids conjunctive order by placing the pronoun next to the verb, e.g.

1242	setton him to heafdon	hilderandas
2430	heold mec ond hæfde	Hreðel cyning,

though the conjunctive order 'him hilderandas to heafdon setton' 'mec Hreðel cyning heold ond hæfde' would be equally good metrically. The conclusion therefore seems irresistible that the two types of co-ordinate clause (the asyndetic and that introduced by *ond*) were alternatives, that each was used in its proper context, and that, in poetry as in prose, the type with conjunctive order could only stand after *ond* and was never asyndetic. With or without *ond*, the sentences cited in 97 can only be co-ordinate clauses.

100. There are, however, some apparently similar sentence-forms with conjunctive order for which a different explanation must be sought, e.g.

Beo. 925   [Hroðgar maðelode,] he to healle geong
    1215   [Wealhðeo maðelode,] heo fore þæm werede spræc
    2724   [Beowulf maðelode,] he ofer benne spræc
    3163   [wealle beworhton...bronde lafe.]
          Hi on beorg dydon   beg ond siglu

These are all evidently co-ordinate clauses; as however there is no change of subject, the pronoun in each is otiose and unidiomatic. The correct form can be seen in

1687   Hroðgar maðelode,   hylt sceawode

and many similar lines, and the pronouns in the examples cited should be ejected as intruders. In

1994   [Ic ðæs modceare
       sorhwylmum seað,   siðe ne truwode
       leofes mannes;] ic ðe lange bæd

the second 'ic' is again otiose and may be a misreading of 'ac'.

101. There remains one other unusual sentence-form to consider, viz. *Ða ic...gefrægn*. There are five instances of it in *Beowulf* and one or two in each of the poems *Andreas, Exodus, Genesis, Judith*; all of these are pointed by editors as principal sentences. Our rule in Chapter II, however, requires them to be taken as subordinate adverbial clauses, and this construction suits the context in every place, e.g.

Beo. 2752   Ða ic snude gefrægn   sunu Wihstanes
          hyran heaðosiocum...
          Geseah ða sigehreðig...
          'When (as I heard the tale) W.'s son quickly obeyed his
          wounded lord, then saw he [many a costly jewel]'.

Here the principal sentence follows the *ða*-clause, and so in 74, 2484, 2694; it may, however, precede the *ða*-clause, as in

Beo. 2771 Næs þæs wyrmes þær
onsyn ænig   ac hine ecg fornam
Ða ic on hlæwe gefrægn hord reafian | anne mannan
'No sign of dragon was there but sword's edge had taken
him off when (so it was told) one man within the
barrow rifled the hoard'.

Two examples from *Judith* are most instructive:

7   Gefrægn ic ða Olofernus...winhatan wyrcean georne
246   Ða ic ædre gefrægn
slegefæge hæleð   slæpe tobredan...

The first shows that the order of the words in a principal sentence is
not Ða ic gefrægn but, as we should expect, Gefrægn ic ða; the
second is the only place in which our formula occurs in a *b*-verse
and proves conclusively that *ða* is a conjunction, for if *ða* were the
adverb, and therefore stressed, we should have a *b*-verse with the
forbidden three lifts. It may be observed further (i) that the *ic
gefrægn* formula only occurs in *ða*-clauses; in all others the phrase
is *mine gefræge* as in *Beo.* 775 þær fram sylle abeag medubenc
monig mine gefræge; (ii) that a constant feature of the idiom is the
interception between the pronoun and the verb of an adverb or
adverb phrase (wide, on morgne, æt þearfe, snude) which really
belongs to the following infinitive.

CHAPTER XI

PARATAXIS

102. In this chapter we shall consider what is usually called the paratactic structure of Old English. The word Parataxis may be used in two senses; it may mean simply a lack of grammatical subordination such as we find in the language of children and some primitive peoples, or, secondly, it may be a rhetorical device by which a subordinate relation is idiomatically expressed by a co-ordinately juxtaposed sentence, as when we say 'Knock and it shall be opened' instead of 'If ye knock, it shall be opened'. It is in the first of these two senses that many speak of Old English as paratactic; they are thinking of something immature and almost childish, as in the sentences

Then I asked him; then he replied...
They came to a place on the road; there stood a temple.
There lived in the convent a certain monk; he was called Martin: he said....

Now it is true that in certain OE prose writings, e.g. the earlier parts of the *Chronicle*, this kind of parataxis is to be found, but our investigations have shown that it is an error to think it characteristic of OE style at any period, either in prose or verse; we have seen that many of the supposed forms of principal sentence can really only be subordinate, while on the other hand some possible forms of principal sentence are ambiguous, i.e. may equally well be dependent clauses.

103: Let us now consider the second kind of parataxis mentioned above, viz. when it is idiomatically used to indicate subordination. In this sense, every language has its own characteristic parataxis besides some forms of it which appear to be common to all languages alike; we shall here describe the forms peculiar to Old, when contrasted with Modern, English:

(i) A paratactic sentence, usually introduced by *wolde, wende* or cwæð, is equivalent to an adverbial clause of Reason or Purpose, e.g.

Hom. II. 32. 26. Heo eode of ðam stæpum to ðam halgan cyðere, wolde hi gebiddan 'She went from the steps to the holy martyr in order to pray'.

I. 462. 11. ðone ðe ða Judeiscan on rode ahengon: wendon þæt se deað hine gehæftan mihte 'whom the Jews hanged on a cross, thinking that death might hold him captive'.

I. 366 ft. Hi gelyfdon on manega oðre gesceafta: cwædon þæt hi for heora fægernysse godas wæron 'They believed in many other creatures, saying that they were Gods because of their beauty'.

As poetic usage is just the same, it may be illustrated here from *Beowulf*:

1339   ond nu oðer cwom
      mihtig manscaða,   wolde hyre mæg wrecan.
      'and now has come a second strong enemy to avenge her son'.

2239   ond se an ða gen
      wearð winegeomor: wende ðæs ylcan
      'and the survivor went grieving for his friends, expecting
      the same fate'.

2158   sume worde het
      þæt ic his ærest ðe   est gesægde;
      cwæð þæt hit hæfde   Hiorogar cyning
      'bade me mention the gift of armour first because King
      Herogar once possessed it'.

The verb in all such paratactic clauses stands first, and the subject, if unchanged, is normally unexpressed. Not infrequently instead of a single verb we have a hendiadys, e.g. *Bede* 232 ft. woldon ond wilnadan, 308. 11 woldon ond wendon, *Beo.* 1604 wiscton ond [ne] wendon. Very occasionally we have two paratactic sentences in sequence, e.g.

Hom. II. 518. 20. Pictavienscisce þearle wiðcwædon: woldon hab-ban ðone ylcan þe hi ær alændon to ðam biscopdome, cwædon þæt he wære heora munuc æt fruman 'The Poitevins stoutly resisted in order to retain the man they had given to the bishopric, saying that he had originally been their monk'.

It will be observed that paratactic 'wolde' introduces what is virtually a final clause. Verbs other than the three mentioned are not common, but they are found, e.g.

Hom. I. 414. 17. He wand swa swa wurm: ne mihte geðolian þa egeslican gesihðe ðæra awyrgedra gasta 'He was turning like a worm, not being able to endure the dreadful sight of the accursed spirits'.

104. (ii) The paratactic sentence is equivalent to a defining clause; here also the verb is the head-word with subject unexpressed, e.g.

ASC 1012. and hine þær bysmorlice acwylmdon: oftorfedon mid banum ond hryþera heafdum 'and there they killed him ignominiously, pelting him with bones and oxen's heads'.

Bede 52. 24. ond sona ða beotunge dædum gefyldon: bærndon ond hergedon ond slogan 'and at once carried out their threat, burning and harrying and slaying'.

Oros. 17. 9. Ða for he norþryhte be þam lande: let him þæt weste land on þæt steorbord 'Then he went North along the land, leaving the uninhabited land on his starboard'.

This type of parataxis is particularly common after 'swa don' or the like, e.g.

ASC 896. onð hie þa swa dydon: worhton ða tu geweorc on twa healfe 'and they did so, building two forts, one on either bank'.

Hom. II. 138. 7. Ða dyde he swa his gewuna wæs, sang his gebedu 'Then he did according to his wont, singing his prayers...'.

Beo. 538   ond þæt geæfndon swa.
        Hæfdon swurd nacod þa wit on sund reon
        'and achieved our boast, carrying our swords unsheathed
        as we swam'.

105. (iii) The paratactic sentence is equivalent to a comparative clause, e.g.

Hom. II. 574. 1. hi sind oðre oðre hi wæron 'they are other than they were'.

Oros. 288. 16. onfunde þæt he on oðran geleafan wære on oðran he self wæs 'discovered that he believed differently from himself'.

106. (iv) The paratactic sentence is equivalent to an Adjectival clause or phrase, e.g.

Boet. 1. ða wæs sum consul. Boetius wæs haten 'there was at the time a consul called Boetius'.

Oros. 140. 15. Ða bæd his fæder—wæs eac Favius haten— 'Then his father, also called Fabius, begged...'.

The verb is usually *hatan*, but others are occasionally found, e.g.

ASC 906. Her gefor Ælfred, wæs æt Baðum gerefa 'In this year Alfred, the reeve at Bath, died'.

It is remarkable that 'hatte' should be occasionally found attached
to a noun in an oblique case, e.g.

Oros. 66. 31. He læg mid Latinus wife, Lucretia hatte 'He lay with
Lucretia, Latinus' wife'.

Bede 28. 26. mid heora heretogan Reada hatte 'with their leader,
whose name was Reada',

the more usual construction with an oblique case being the
participle 'haten'.

107. Before leaving these paratactic sentences we ought to ask
ourselves how they should be punctuated: punctuation as we
understand it is absent in the MSS., but the examples, especially
in (i) and (ii), show that our texts, as pointed by modern editors,
usually separate the paratactic from the principal verb by a colon
or full-stop and make two sentences. Now all the forms of parataxis are found *within* the subordinate clause, e.g.

LS 30. 329. Ða cyrde he eft ongean, wolde feccan me, þa com an
wulf ond gelæhte mine broðor 'When he returned in order to fetch me,
there came a wolf and seized my brother'.

CP 256. 19. þæt he spræc oðer oðer he sprecan wolde 'that he spoke
other than he intended'.

Hom. II. 156. 2. þær hine afedde sum eawfæst munuc, Romanus
hatte 'where a pious monk, called Romanus, fed him'.

In any of these sentences a colon or full-stop disintegrates the
clause, and is not to be thought of. There can be little doubt,
therefore, that the appropriate punctuation is a comma; and so
also in the forms of parataxis common to Old and Modern English,
e.g. where we have a Jussive subjunctive:

Hom. I. 256. 14. Gif rice wif and earm acennað togædere, gangon hi
aweig; nast ðu hwæðer bið ðæs rican wifes cild 'If a rich woman and a
poor one bring forth together, suppose they go away, you do not know
which is the rich woman's child'.

Replace the semicolon after 'aweig' by a comma.

108. The idiom we have just been considering affords no ground
at all for asserting that the general syntactical structure of OE
prose was lacking in subordination. Even in the earliest prose
every kind of subordinate clause is to be found, and, if the composition is often clumsy, that is the fault of the writer and not of

his instrument; in the mature prose of Ælfric we have a style rich, varied and finely articulated, which moves with ease and precision, as any reader can judge for himself. Let us illustrate, very briefly, some of the weaknesses of OE prose, and by way of contrast give some examples of the stylistic mastery of Ælfric. The chief weakness, if we ignore the demonstrative over-emphasis of certain parts of the *Chronicle*, is a monotony caused by failure to use the varied resources of the language. Take temporal clauses, for example; in those parts of the *Chronicle* where the writer has a larger field and greater narrative scope than in the usual short annalistic records, though there is no lack of subordination, the single conjunction *þa* has usually to do all the duties of Latin cum, postquam, simul ac, dum, etc.: *siððan, ðenden, mid ðam ðe, þa hwile ðe* do not occur at all before the latest entries and *þa furðum* (or *sona swa*) is exceedingly rare. Even the moving story of the Danish wars (872–897) has no conjunction but *þa* or its pleonastic forms except for one example of *sona swa* and one of *ða furðum*; and the monotony is increased by the fact that *ða* is the usual adverb also and that correlation is frequent. The same may be said of OE *Bede*. Let us use that work, however, to illustrate another limitation, viz. the rarity of apposition and other forms of the adjectival phrase, a rarity which is quite remarkable when we consider the extensive use of apposition in OE poetry; the *Bede* translator depends almost entirely on relative clauses, of which there are sometimes three or four together after the same antecedent. Now it must be admitted that Old English, like some other languages, e.g. Ancient Greek, was less sensitive than Modern English to this kind of repetition, but the relative pronoun was not as a rule repeated more than once in idiomatic prose, e.g.

Hom. I. 58 ft. sum wælhreow casere se wæs Domicianus gehaten: se het afyllan ane cyfe mid weallendum ele 'a cruel Emperor called Domitian who ordered a vat to be filled with boiling oil...'.

In *Bede*, however, we have within a dozen pages these three passages, each with at least three relative clauses, as the punctuation ought to show:

230. 13. þæs biscopes broðor se wæs Cælin haten; se wæs mæssepreost ond Godes mon til: se him ond his hiwan godcunde lare gelærde.

This helpless repetition is astonishing when we compare the variety of the Latin original 'fratrem ejusdem episcopi vocabulo Caelin, virum aeque Deo devotum, qui ipsi et familiae ministrare solebat'.

236. 13. in þæm wæs Æðelhere se æfter him to rice feng; se wæs ordfruma ðæs gefeohtes. Þone mon slog... 'in quibus Aedilheri, qui post eum regnavit, auctor ipse belli, interemptus est'.

254. 15. Wæs in þa tid sum munuc in Rome se wæs cuð Adriane, þæs noma wæs Theodorus. Se wæs acenned in Tarso Cilicio.

Here, instead of the Latin, we cite a similar passage from Ælfric to show the difference in style; *Hom.* II. 96. 19 He cwæð þæt he cuðe sumne man on Romebyrig, his nama wæs Servulus, ðearfa on æhtum and welig on geearnungum. Se læg bedryda fram cildhade (so T.; the full-stop should be a comma). 'He said that he knew a man in Rome called Servulus, poor in worldly possessions but rich in merit, who lay bedridden from childhood'. The translator of *Orosius* at his best, which is when he is rendering his Latin freely, comes closest to Ælfric: in narrative especially (Cyrus's Scythian expedition in Sweet's *Reader* is a good example) he has the combined simplicity and variety of Herodotus, and much of his charm. When construing closely he is often laboured in style, e.g. 286. 29 Ða wæs he sume niht on anum niwcilctan huse. Ða het he betan micel fyr.... Ða ongan se cealc mid ungemete stincan; ða wearð Jovianus mid þæm bræðe ofsmored (so Sweet punctuates). Put commas after 'huse' and 'stincan'; the Latin has Cum in cubiculum quoddam novum sese recepisset, calore pruinarum et nidore parietum nuper calce illitorum suffocatus vitam finivit, and the OE translation means 'Being one night in a newly plastered house, he ordered a large fire to be lighted; and as the lime gave off an inordinate stench, Jovian was suffocated by the fumes'. Even so, the double *þa*-correlation so close together is, by Ælfric's standard, heavy and monotonous.

109. Of Ælfric it is impossible to give any real impression by short extracts; the reader should study his *Homilies* as a whole. I content myself here with a few passages from this work, which illustrate both Ælfric's mastery of syntactical construction (not

always apparent in the traditional punctuation) and the masculine
vigour of his style:

I. 52. 5. Þider ðe Stephanus forestop mid Saules stanum oftorfod,
ðider folgode Paulus gefultumod þurh Stephanes gebedu. Ðær nis
Paulus gescynd þurh Stephanes slege, ac Stephanus gladað on Paules
gefærrædene; forðan þe seo soðe lufu on heora ægðrum blissað.

This is really a single period: 'Where Stephen went before, stoned
to death by Saul, thither Paul followed supported by Stephen's
prayers, in which sequence of events Paul is not shamed by
Stephen's murder but Stephen rather is happy in Paul's fellowship,
since true love rejoices in both of them.'

I. 336. 5. Nu cwæð se halga Gregorius þæt sum arwurðe munuc wæs
on ðam earde Licaonia swiðe eawfæst, his nama wæs Martirius. Se
ferde be his abbudes hæse to sumum oðrum mynstre on his ærende: ða
gemette he be wege sumne licðrowere licgende eal tocinen and(?)
nahte his feðes geweald: cwæð þæt he wolde genealæcan his hulce gif
he mihte.

Again one period, containing a relative clause, a þa-clause of the
type discussed in 38, and two kinds of parataxis: 'Now St Gregory
tells us that there was a reverend monk called Martyr in Lycaonia,
very pious, who was going on some errand to another monastery at
his abbot's request when he found by the wayside a leper chapped
with sores all over and unable to move a foot to reach his hut as he
wished.'

I. 390 ft. He wolde forfleon syrewunge Judeiscre ðeode and geðafode
þæt hine man on anre wilian ofer ðone weall nyðer alet: na þæt he
nolde for Cristes geleafan deað þrowian ac forði he forfleah ðone
ungeripedan deað forðan þe he sceolde ærest menigne mann mid his
micclum wisdome to Gode gestrynan.

Here we have a good example of the *forðan* correlation discussed
in 37: 'He wished to escape from the machinations of the Jews and
consented to be let down from the wall in a basket, not because he
was unwilling to suffer death for his faith—the reason why he
shunned a premature death was that he had first to win to God
many a man by his great wisdom.' Thorpe, in his translation,
makes the *forði* sentence subordinate and the *forðan* clause a
principal sentence.

II. 18. 26. þa wæron þær ðry cnihtas swiðe gelyfede on ðone soðan
God: þa wæron gehatene Annanias, Azarias, Misahel. Ða gecwædon

þæt hi noldon bugan to nanum deofolgilde fram heora Scyppende. Ða cwæð se cyning him to 'Hwæt is se God þe mæge eow ahreddan of minum handum?' Ða cwædon hi....

Two sentences, not five: 'There were at that time three youths called Ananias, Azarias and Misael, steadfastly believing in the true God, who resolved not to be false to their Creator or bow to any idol. And when the King asked them "Who is the God that can deliver you out of my hands?" they replied....' Where is the 'paratactic' structure in any one of the passages, even those from *Bede*, which we have so far considered, if they are rightly construed?

110. It is now time to turn to the problem of parataxis in poetry. In Old English, as in many other languages, poetry was the earliest form of literary composition, and one particular kind of poetry, the Epic, reached its zenith almost before prose had begun to be written. Partly for this reason, but even more because of its supposed paratactic structure, the OE epic style, especially in *Beowulf*, has been described as archaic or primitive; there could be no greater delusion. Abundant proof has already been given that the epithet 'paratactic', in the sense in which it is intended, is even less true as a description of syntactical form in *Beowulf* than we have shown it to be in prose; let us, therefore, instead of going again over ground already covered, consider some supposed instances of parataxis from the point of view of style, and, first of all, four which illustrate the poet's skill in managing his transitions:

194   Ðæt fram ham gefrægn   Higelaces þegn,
             god mid Geatum,   Grendles dæda;
             se wæs moncynnes   mægenes strengest...
             æþele ond eacen.   Het him yðlidan
             godne gegyrwan

Since the word-order (51) tolerates *þæt* only as a relative pronoun, and a relative pronoun, at the beginning of a new paragraph, is meaningless, read *þa* for *þæt*, and make the clause subordinate to the following sentence. We have been told in the preceding eighty lines of Grendel's attacks on Hart and of the despair of Hroðgar and his Danes; the stage is therefore set for the hero's entrance, and the poet continues: 'When in his distant home Higelac's thane, famous among the Geats, strongest in might among mankind, heard tell of Grendel's doings, he bade prepare a goodly ship....'

229   Ða of wealle geseah   weard Scildinga,
se þe holmclifu   healdan sceolde,
beran ofer bolcan   beorhte randas...
Gewat him þa to waroðe   wicge ridan.

The order again shows that the first sentence is subordinate, and the clause marks the transition to a fresh scene. The voyage and the landing on Danish soil have just been described and 'When from the cliff the guard whose duty was to watch the coast saw bright shields borne along the gangway, he straightway came riding to the shore...'. Let us now take two examples of transition by means of the 'þa wæs' type, which, as we have seen (19 (ii)), is ambiguous, i.e. may be either principal or subordinate:

126   Ða wæs on uhtan   mid ærdæge
Grendles guðcræft   gumum undyrne;
þa wæs æfter wiste   wop up ahafen.

The first assault on Hart, in which Grendel carried off thirty thanes, has just been described, and the poet continues: 'When at dawn, with break of day, Grendel's fighting-power was made manifest to men, then after feasting was lamentation raised'; the correlation is obvious, and two 'thens' are as intolerable here as they would be in Lady Macbeth's 'When you durst do it, then you were a man'. For the conventional stress on the conjunction *þa* at the beginning of a line, cf.

2204   þa hyne gesohtan   on sigeþeode
hearde hildfrecan....

3134   þa wæs wunden gold   on wæn hladen,
aeghwæs unrim,   æþeling boren,
har hilderinc,   to Hrones Næsse.
Him ða gegiredan   Geata leode
ad on eorðan.

These lines introduce the last scene of all, the hero's burning and burial; the bier has been made ready, the hoard brought out of the barrow, and the dragon shoved over the sea-cliff, and 'When the twisted gold had been loaded on a wain, and the atheling borne to the Whale's Ness, then did the Geat-folk prepare for him a pyre...'.

There is nothing 'primitive' about these transitions; they are as artfully contrived as any in later English poetry.

111. Let us now consider a few examples of supposed parataxis where we have really correlation by means of adverbs other than demonstrative, e.g. *nu, siððan, swa*:

424   ond nu wið Grendel sceal,
        wið þam aglæcan,   ana gehegan
        ðing wið þyrse.   Ic þe nu ða,
        brego Beorht-Dena,   biddan wille....

The sense itself suggests correlation and metre requires it unless it can be proved either that the first *nu* could be unstressed as an adverb, or (if it be stressed) that metrical practice tolerated three lifts in a *b*-verse; making the two sentences one, we have 'and since by my single hand I (?) must settle accounts with the monster Grendel, I would now beg of thee, Prince of the Bright-Danes, one boon...'.

2070   þæt ðu geare cunne,
        sinces brytta,   to hwan syððan wearð
        hondræs hæleða.   Syððan heofones gim
        glad ofer grundas,   gæst yrre cwom

Again the juxtaposition suggests correlation and again metre supports it, for the second 'syððan' must be unstressed and therefore a conjunction for the same reasons as in the preceding instance. Correlate the two sentences and we have 'that thou mayst know what was the issue of the struggle after heaven's jewel had glided from over the plain and the monster came in wrath...'.

3066   Swa wæs Biowulfe   þa he biorges weard
        sohte searoniða...
        Swa hit oð domes dæg   diore benemdon.

Two So's here are meaningless; for what sense can be attached to the first 'so' except as defined by the correlative just below? 'It befell Beowulf according to the curse which the great ones had solemnly pronounced...'.

112. We shall now examine some passages from *Beowulf* which illustrate the great variety of its periodic structure (in each one the traditional punctuation is given):

461   ða hine Wedera cyn
        for herebrogan   habban ne mihte.
        Đanon he gesohte   Suð-Dena folc
        ofer yða gewealc,   Ar-Scyldinga.
        Đa ic furþum weold   folce Deniga
                          ...Đa wæs Heregar dead,
        bearn Healfdenes;   se wæs betera ðonne ic.

This is a passage which is crucial for the syntax and style of the
poem; the first two *þa*-sentences (19 (i)) must be subordinate and
the third may be, while *se*, not being an antecedent, must (48) be
a relative and not a demonstrative pronoun. There are, therefore,
not five principal sentences, but one; and the sense is what the
context requires: 'When the Weder-folk through fear of war might
hold him not, thence sought he the South-Dane people at the time
when I began to rule them, since Heregar, Healfden's heir, was
dead, who was a better man than I.' Here is the translation of the
traditional text: 'Then the race of the Weders would not receive
him because of threatening war. Thence he sought the people of
the South-Danes over the surge of the waves. Then I had just
begun to rule the Danish people and in youth held a wide-stretched
kingdom....Then Heregar was dead, the son of Healfden: he was
better than I' (R. K. Gordon in *Everyman*). I am not criticizing
Gordon's translation, which is an exact rendering of his text; but
can anyone believe that such a string of emphatic demonstrative
sentences truly represents the genius of OE poetry?

        [Se þe wæteregesan   wunian scolde]
1261   ...siþðan Cain wearð
        to ecgbanan   angan breþer,
        fæderenmæge: he þa fag gewat
        morþre gemearcod   mandream fleon,
        westen warode.   Đanon woc fela
        geosceaftgasta;

These three sentences again form a single period. Sense requires
the *siððan*-clause to be subordinated to the following sentence and
not the preceding one: 'after Cain had killed his own brother,
branded with murder he went, far from the joys of men, to dwell in
the wild—Cain, from whom were born many doomed spirits...'.
The usual translation 'Who (i.e. Grendel's mother) was doomed to

dwell in dread waters after Cain killed his only brother' is feeble, since she was still unborn at the time.

1376
            Nu is se ræd gelang
    eft æt þe anum.   Eard git ne const,
    frecne stowe,   þær þu findan miht
    fela-sinnigne secg: sec gif þu dyrre

For metrical reasons *nu* must be unstressed and therefore a conjunction, and sense requires the second sentence to be taken as an asyndetic clause co-ordinate to the first. This construction is confirmed by the imperative in the principal sentence (36 (ii)); the meaning is 'Since help again is in thee alone, and thou knowest not yet the lair, the fearsome place, where thou mayst find the miscreant, seek it if thou dare'.

2442
            sceolde hwæðre swaþeah
    æðeling unwrecen   ealdres linnan.
    Swa bið geomorlic   gomelum ceorle
    to gebidanne   þæt his byre ride
    giong on galgan;   þonne he gyd wrece,
    sarigne sang,   þonne his sunu hangað....

The *Everyman* translation has: 'Yet in spite of that the chieftain must needs pass from life unavenged. In like manner it is sad for an aged man to endure that his son in his youth should swing from the gallows. Then he makes a measure, a song of sorrow, when his son hangs....' What sense can be made of the middle sentence? *Swa* has its idiomatic causal sense, as in 881; and the only syntax which can justify the order after *þonne* and the mood of 'wrece' (27) is that which makes the sentence co-ordinate to the preceding one. The meaning is 'Yet for all that the atheling must needs lose his life unavenged, seeing that it is a grievous thing for an old man to endure that his young son should ride on gallows and he himself utter his dirge, his song of sorrow, when his heir is hanging, a joy to ravens'.

113. We conclude this survey with two examples of *ða*-correlation in which there is an intervening co-ordinate clause wrongly called paratactic:

2715
        Ða se æðeling giong
    [þæt he] gesæt on sesse;   seah on enta geweorc
    hu ða stanbogan   stapulum fæste

ece eorðreced   innan heolde.
Hyne þa mid handa...   þegn ungemete till
winedryhten his   wætere gelafede.

The traditional text takes this as three principal sentences meaning 'Then the chieftain went....He looked on the work of giants....Then the good thane bathed him'; the first sentence, however, must be a subordinate clause, 'seah on' (note the subjectless verb) co-ordinate to it and 'Hyne ða...' the correlated principal sentence. Further, 2716–18 is usually translated 'looked on the work of giants (i.e. the masonry) how the earth-building held within stone arches'; but in all the other places in *Beowulf* where giants' handiwork is mentioned it means metal-work (swords, ornaments, etc.) and there can be little doubt that it means the same here: 'looked on the treasure, giants' handiwork, and beheld how the pillared arches, the enduring earth-chamber, guarded it within.' This interpretation is confirmed by 2756 Geseah ða sigehreðig ða he bi sesse geong gold glitinian, where Wihstan from the very same point of view (the *sess*) also sees the treasure.

1896   Þa wæs on sande   sægeap naca
hladen herewædum....   Mæst hlifade
ofer Hroðgares   hordgestreonum.
He þa[m] batwearde   bunden golde
swurd gesealde

The traditional text again punctuates this as three principal sentences: 'Then was the broad-beamed ship laden with battlegear; the mast rose high above H.'s hoard-gifts; then he gave, etc.' 'Ða wæs' certainly tolerates this construction but it is better taken as a subordinate clause, for, since the sentence before has told how the watchman met the Geats and welcomed them to the ship, the transition is characteristic: 'When the ship was laden [and] the mast set up above the gifts (i.e. when all was ready for departure), then gave he to the shipwarden a gold-mounted sword.' The periodic structure is just the same as in the preceding example, the second sentence being co-ordinate to the first and both subordinate to the third; 'þam' (þā) is (68) a misreading of 'þa'.

114. *Beowulf* is usually regarded as the grand example of the OE paratactic style. If we add together all the supposed principal

sentences in the poem which are really either subordinate or co-ordinate clauses and the ambiguous sentences which are preferably taken as subordinate, we have a total of over 260, and the traditional text, if rightly punctuated, is quite transformed by the addition of 260 new dependent clauses, which is at the rate of one in every twelve lines. Nothing in fact is left of the supposed paratactic style; except for the occasional use of idiomatic parataxis, itself as we have seen (103 *sqq*.) a subordinating device, the prevailing sentence-structure is not paratactic at all but periodic.

CHAPTER XII

THE FORMS OF THE OLD ENGLISH RELATIVE PRONOUN

115. The simplest forms of the OE relative pronoun are *ðe* and *se*. We have shown (41) that the former is used when the relative clause has the function of a distinguishing or limiting adjective, and the latter when it has the function of a descriptive adjective; see the examples there given. In this chapter we shall discuss some variant forms of these two relative pronouns.

116. We begin with *se*; this is the regular form, but in late prose *seðe* (*ðæs ðe, ðæm ðe*, etc.) begins to prevail, e.g.

Hom. I. 28. 22. mid Gode seðe ana on ecnysse rixað 'with God, who alone rules eternally'.

I. 96 ft. þu bist geciged niwum naman þone ðe Godes muð genemnode 'Thou shalt be called by a new name which God's mouth has named'.

This pronoun must be distinguished grammatically from a form which at first sight appears to be the same, e.g.

ASC 46A. Herodes se þe Jacobum ofslog 'Herod, the one who slew James'.

Bede 136. 11. be þam Gode þam ðe he bodade 'about the God whom he preached'.

In these, *se* and *þam* are not part of the relative pronoun but are the usual demonstrative antecedent, which repeats epexegetically the noun antecedent 'Herodes' or 'Gode'; such an analysis is impossible in the Ælfric examples since *se* and *þone* do not agree in case with the noun antecedents 'Gode' and 'naman'. How then are we to explain the forms *seðe* and *þone ðe*? They can only be the relative pronouns *se* and *þone* with a relative particle *ðe* suffixed to them, just as *ðider ðe, ðonon ðe*, etc., are common forms of the relative adverbs in Ælfric, e.g. *Hom.* I. 52. 5 Þider ðe Stephanus forestop ðider folgode Paulus 'Whither S. went before, thither P. followed'; no doubt the convenience of being able to distinguish the demonstrative from the relative pronoun or adverb accounts for the innovation. That this is the right explanation is confirmed by the fact that this new relative pronoun is in Ælfric always written as one word *seðe* in the nominative singular and frequently as *ðaðe* in the nominative plural. (So at least in C, the best MS.; Sweet's *ASR* xiii and xiv has *se ðe* in places, perhaps from R or B.)

117. We have thus three forms of the descriptive relative pronoun, viz.:

(i) the simple form *se* (*þæs, þæm,* etc.);

(ii) the pleonastic form *seðe* (*ðaðe, þæs ðe, þæm· ðe,* etc.) in which *ðe* is a suffix to the unstressed relative *se*;

(iii) the epanaleptic form *sé ðe* (*þæs ðe, ðæm ðe,* etc.) in which *se* is the usual stressed antecedent and *ðe* the normal relative pronoun after it. It will be convenient to speak of (ii) as the *seðe* form and of (iii) as the *se ðe* form. Both occur sporadically in all late OE prose, but in some texts one or the other is found almost exclusively: we may take the *Rushworth* Gospels as an example of a *se ðe* text and the *Lindisfarne* Gospels as an example of a *seðe* text. Here are some instructive parallels from *St Matthew*:

	Rushworth	*Lindisfarne*
vi. 1.	mid eower fæder þæne þe in heofonum is	mid fader iurre seðe in heafnas is
vi. 18.	þinum fæder ðæm ðe in degulnisse is	federe þinum se ðe is in degolnisse
vii. 15.	wið lease witgu (*acc.*) þa þe cumað to eow	from leasum witgum ðaðe cymes to iuh
vii. 26.	gelic were dysig þæm þe timbrade hus	se ðe getimberde hus

Cf. also vii. 21, 24; viii. 33; x. 32; xiii. 24. It will be observed that *Lindisfarne* sometimes writes *seðe* as *se ðe* (two words).

118. Let us now attempt to classify the principal OE prose writings according to the prevailing form of *se* in each:

(i) *se*-texts: the best example is the *Chronicle* which has only four *seðe* forms in all the A and E entries up to A.D. 1000; three of these may quite well be the *se ðe* form, viz. 46 A, already cited, and

81 A. Titus seþe sæde þæt he þone dæg forlure. . . .
827 A. se eahteþa cyning seþe Bretwalda wæs. . . .

where E has *se þe* ('Titus, he who said that he lost the day. . .').
The only unambiguous *seðe* form is in

984 A. Ælfheages (*gen.*) seðê oðrum naman wæs Godwine

and even the long E document as late as 1005–1036 has only *se*
forms. *Orosius* is another *se*-text with a few *seðe* or *se þe* forms,
some of which may be epexegetic, e.g.

32. 29. Joseph, se þe gingst wæs hys gebroðra 'Joseph, the one who
was the youngest brother'.
70. 1. Gesetton hirran ladteow þone þe hie tictator heton 'They
established a higher magistrate, the one they called dictator'.

Bede, on the whole, is a *se*-text; in the first 200 pages there are
ninety-seven instances of *se*, thirty of *seðe* (frequently written
se ðe), sixty-three of *þæs*, *þæm*, etc., and only nine of *þæs ðe*,
þæm ðe, etc. Of the epexegetic *se þe* there are six instances in an
oblique case, e.g.

174. 14. Monige þara broðra þara ðe in oðrum husum wæron 'Many
of the brothers who were in other houses'.

The comparatively wide variety of forms in *Bede* may be due to
the frequent change of scribe (see Miller's Introduction). Rather
frequently in *Bede*, and rarely in *Orosius*, we have *se þe (seðe)* in
the sense of *ðe*; this use will be discussed later.

(ii) *seðe* texts: the only work in which *seðe* in all cases and
numbers is used with some consistency is the Lindisfarne *Gospels*
in the Durham Book, already quoted. Ælfric, both in the *Homilies*
and the *Lives of the Saints*, has it only in the nominative; for the
oblique cases he uses generally the simple forms *ðæs*, *ðæm*, etc. In
the first 200 pages of *Hom.* I. there are sixty-four instances of *seðe*
to twenty of *se*, but only five of *þam ðe*, etc., to thirty-three of
ðæm; it is noteworthy, however, that older documents used in the
Homilies (e.g. the Creeds) have only *se* and never *seðe*. The usage
of the West-Saxon *Gospels* and of *CP* agrees with that of Ælfric,
except that *CP* has a relatively greater number of *ðæs ðe* forms.

(iii) *se ðe* texts: the only work in which the *se ðe* form, in both
the nominative and the oblique cases, is used with consistency is

the Rushworth *Gospels* (see examples 117); but it may occur in a proper context in *se-* or *seðe*-texts also.

119. In most late writings sporadic instances occur of *seðe* as a form not of *se* but of *ðe* (e.g. se mann seðe geliefð 'the man that believes') and in some they abound. Ælfric has *seðe* in this sense after a noun with the definite article, but never immediately after the pronoun antecedent (se seðe) though he admits 'se ylca seðe' (I. 20. 16) and 'gehwa seðe' (188. 24). The *Chronicle* never has the form at all in the A or E text. In *Orosius* se se þe occurs six times, e.g. 84. 12 se se þe ær geþuhte, 210. 6 se se þe cristen næs, but in five of the six Bosworth, following C, the better MS., reads the normal *se þe*. In *Bede* some of the thirty *seðe* forms mentioned above introduce a limiting clause (= *ðe*); here also it is significant that other MSS. have variants for several of them. In *CP* the form *se se þe* is frequent. We must conclude that, although in some of these texts *seðe* (= *ðe*) cannot be regarded as certified, the fact that it occurs in almost all of them is strong evidence that scribes of the late period were accustomed to it. How then did it originate? Perhaps from the epexegetic *se ðe* which occasionally introduces a limiting clause, e.g.

Hom. I. 38. 11. on eorðan sibb mannum ðam þe beoð godes willan 'on earth peace to men [those] that are of good will'

(whereas just above the same limiting clause has its usual form: 38. 2 on eorðan sibb þam mannum þe beoð etc.). Is it not possible that in a sentence like Preostas þa ðe Læden cunnon (=priests [those] that know Latin) the *ðá ðe* was misread as *ðaðe* and then the *seðe* form (= *ðe*) became general for all cases of the pronoun?

120. Almost all the examples hitherto have been from West-Saxon texts and can, therefore, only be taken as certifying the linguistic usage of that dialect. Is there any evidence for the other dialects? We have seen that the E version of the *Chronicle* has only the simplest forms of the relative pronoun; it is likely that much of it was written in an Anglian or Mercian district, but the problem of its composition is too complicated to admit of any certain conclusions. We have, however, one important Mercian document in the Rushworth version of *St Matthew*; in this, as we

have seen, the usual form of *se* is the epexegetic *se ðe*, but the limiting relative has almost always the simple form *ðe* both after the demonstrative antecedent, e.g. vii. 8 se þe soeceþ, viii. 33 be þæm þe deofulseoke werun, and after other words, e.g. vii. 14 se weg þe lædeþ to life, vii. 23 ge þe wyrcaþ unrihtnisse, vii. 26 æghwilc þe gehereð, though the WS form 'ælc (æghwilc) ðara ðe' with sing. verb has begun to appear. Finally, the Mercian and Kentish ninth-century Charters have *se* and *ðe* almost without exception.

121. This survey would not be complete without some observations on the forms of the relative pronoun in OE verse; for reasons of space we shall take our examples chiefly from *Beowulf*. The poem is remarkable for a mixture of types and a grammatical licence in the use of them to which no parallel can be found in any prose work. Of the simple form *se* there are thirty-one instances and of the oblique cases *þæs, þæm*, etc., twenty-four; the pleonastic forms are almost as numerous, *seðe* occurring forty-two times, *þæm ðe*, etc., eight, and *þaðe* (nom. pl.) three; and the epexegetic forms (*þóne ðe*, etc.) number twenty-two. It is deserving of remark that though all our printed texts give *se ðe* and *ða ðe* for the nom. sing. and pl. of the pleonastic form, Zupitza's facsimile shows that the MS. has *seðe* and *ðaðe*; there are perhaps three places in which *se ðe* is a possible reading.

122. So much for the forms; let us now look at some constructions. The limiting clauses which have the epexegetic form *þara ðe* number eighteen, and nine of them show a false concord, viz.

842	secga ænegum	
	þara þe tirleases	trode sceawode
996	secga gehwylcum	þara þe on swylc starað
1051	[æghwylcum] þara þe mid Beowulfe	brimlade teah
1406	þone selestan	
	þara þe mid Hroðgare	ham eahtode
1461	manna ængum	þara þe hit mid mundum bewand
1685	ðæm selestan	
	ðara þe on Scedenigge	sceattas dælde
2129	hreowa tornost	
	þara þe leodfruman	lange begeate
2250	fyra gehwylcne	
	leoda minra	þara ðe þis lif ofgeaf
2382	þone selestan	sæcyninga
	þara ðe in Swiorice	sinc brytnade

In all these the singular verb with a plural subject arouses suspicion. Elsewhere in *Beowulf* 'gehwylc þara ðe' is followed by a plural verb, as in

98	cynna gehwylcum	þara ðe cwice hwyrfaþ
784		anra gehwylcum
	þara þe of wealle	wop gehyrdon

and the singular in 996, 2251 looks like a reminiscence on the part of the scribe of the late WS construction after *ælc þara ðe*. In four of the examples (1406, 1686, 2130, 2383) there is a superlative, and the unambiguous form 'begeate' (2131) makes it likely that the mood in the other three is also a subjunctive, which is the regular OE idiom in a clause following a comparative or superlative adjective. Now we can say either 'hreowa tornost þe leodfruman lange begeate = the sorest grief that beset H. for years' (cf. *Gen.* 627 wifa wlitegost ðe on woruld come) or 'hreowa tornost þara þe hine lange begeaton (*indic.*) = 'the sorest of the griefs that had beset H. for years'; but we cannot mix the two constructions. It looks as if our examples were due to a conflation of the two types as elsewhere, e.g.

Guth. 1360   se selesta
       þara þe we on engle   æfre gefrunen
       acennedne
       'the best man that we have ever heard of as born in England.'

where 'acennedne' shows that the antecedent of *þe* must be singular and not plural and certifies *þara* as an interpolation.

123. There are some other solecisms in the *Beowulf* examples we are considering, e.g.

205   Hæfde se goda   Geata leoda
       cempan gecorone   þara þe he cenoste
       findan mihte:
       'He had picked warriors of the Geat-folk, the boldest he could find'.

1122   Lig ealle forswealg,
       gæsta gifrost,   þara ðe þær guð fornam
       'The flame, greediest of spirits, had swallowed up all that war had taken off'.

In both of these we can only refer *þara* to the wrong noun antecedents, Geata (instead of cempan) and gæsta: the result in the latter passage is complete nonsense, yet no other construction is possible unless it can be shown that 'ealle þara' (= all of those) was good OE usage. And what can be the construction of þara in

877   wide siðas
            þara þe gumena bearn   gearwe ne wiston
or in

1625   mægenbyrþenne   þara þe he him mid hæfde

where a noun of reference fails altogether? It appears then that three-quarters of our eighteen *þara ðe* clauses are syntactically irregular in one way or another. This irregularity, however, disappears in all of them if we remove the *þara*; we have seen that after a superlative the simple relative *ðe* is the norm, and the same is true in some texts after *gehwylc*, e.g.

Mald. 128   hyssa gehwylc
            þe on Denon wolde   dom gefeohtan
Jud. 50   on æghwylcne   þe ðærinne com

124. Let us consider our examples for a moment from the metrical point of view. Numerous instances prove that in epexegetic *þara ðe* the demonstrative pronoun is stressed, e.g.

Beo. 1195   healsbeaga mæst,
            þara ðe ic on foldan   gefrægen hæbbe:

this being so, it is remarkable that almost every *b*-verse in which it occurs has at least three stresses and three lifts and sometimes more; 1123 and 2251 (above) have four stresses. It cannot be a coincidence that the same operation which repairs the syntax in all these verses, i.e. the excision of *þara*, also repairs the metre.

125. We now turn to another anomaly in *Beowulf*, the use of pleonastic *seðe* (= *ðe*) in a limiting relative clause. We have seen that this occurs in late West-Saxon prose, though even there it is rare; in *Beowulf* it abounds. We have it after a common or proper noun antecedent with the definite article:

87   se ellorgæst...seþe in þystrum bad
            'the alien spirit that dwelt in darkness'.
506   Eart þu se Beowulf   seþe wið Brecan wunne
            'Art thou the Beowulf that strove with Breca?'

and after a demonstrative antecedent:

1054   ond þone ænne heht   þone ðe Grendel ær
         mane acwealde...
         'and bade payment be made for the one that G. killed'.
1296   Se wæs Hroðgare   hæleþa leofost...
         þone ðe heo on ræste abreat
         'He that she destroyed in his sleep was to H. the dearest of
             men'.

and after 'monig':

908   snotor ceorl monig
         se þe him bealwa to   bote gelyfde
         'many a prudent man that had trusted him for help'.

Now after all three kinds of antecedent the normal relative in
Beowulf, as elsewhere, is *ðe*; and it would be difficult to find either
in prose or verse a parallel to *seðe* after a proper noun with the
article. In some of the instances, moreover, we have the false
concord, this time of gender, which we have learned to expect in
relative clauses in *Beowulf*, e.g.

1259   ides aglæcwif...
         se þe wæteregesan   wunian scolde
1343   nu seo hand ligeð
         se þe eow welhwylcra   wilna dohte
2684   wæs sio hand to strong
         se ðe meca gehwane...swenge ofersohte.

As *seðe* is the wrong relative in all such examples and gives us a
false gender in some of them, the conclusion seems irresistible that
se is an intruder; the simple excision of this syllable makes every
sentence normal. On the other hand, the regular form of the
limiting relative without antecedent was *se*, e.g.

Beo. 142   heold hine syðþan
         fyr ond fæstor   se þæm feonde ætwand;

for this *se*, however, the traditional text has usually WS *seðe*, as
in the very similar sentence

788   Heold hine fæste
         seþe manna wæs   mægene strengest.

This relative occurs normally where the relative clause follows the
principal sentence, and in all periods of English it has been idiomatic
in a jussive sentence (Secge se wille, Catch who can).

126. The most disturbing fact about the relative clauses we have been considering in the last four paragraphs is the appearance in a very early Anglian or Mercian poem of forms and constructions which are probably West-Saxon and certainly late. In both *Judith* and *Maldon*, which have obvious affinities with *Beowulf*, the relative pronouns are of the simplest form: *ðe* alone is used in limiting clauses both after nouns and after the demonstrative antecedent *se*, and *se* is the form in descriptive clauses with the single exception of *þa ðe* in *Jud.* 214. There is no instance in either poem of *þara ðe* even in lines where it would be appropriate, e.g.

Jud. 96   anra gehwylcne
        herbuendra   þe hyne him to helpe seceð

and it may be noted that *Maldon* has the right form after a proper noun with the article

325   næs þæt na se Godric   þe ða guðe forbeah

Moreover, there is as much positive evidence as we can expect that relative pronouns were tampered with. *Brunanburh* (937 *ASC*) is one of the few poems for which there are several MSS.; the one line in which the pronoun-form *þara ðe* occurs (l. 26) has the following variants: B, C hæleþa þara ðe mid Anlafe...land gesohtan, A þæ, D ðe. Similarly, in *Soul's Address*, which survives in two MSS., the V. version of 4 (asyndreð þa sybbe þa ðe ær samod wæron) omits the second *þa*. The most likely explanation is that *ðe* originally stood in both poems but was altered by a scribe to *þara ðe, þa ðe*; which is just what the internal evidence led us to suppose in the *Beowulf* examples.

127. Our conclusions in this chapter may be summed up as follows:

(i) in a limiting relative clause, the relative pronoun is normally *ðe*, as always in *ASC*, though pleonastic *seðe* is found occasionally in late prose but is not always well certified;

(ii) in a descriptive relative clause, there are three forms of the relative pronoun (*a*) unstressed *se*, as always with one exception in *ASC* and predominantly in *Orosius* and *Bede*; (*b*) unstressed *seðe* (=*se* with a relative suffix, cf. ModE 'who that' 'when that') as in Ælfric, *CP*, and WS *Gospels*; in the oblique cases it is only used with any consistency in the Durham Book; (c) epexegetic *se ðe*, where *se* is the stressed antecedent in apposition to a preceding noun; it occurs sporadically in all texts but predominantly only in the Rushworth *St Matthew*. There are good grounds for supposing that *ðe* and *se* were the earliest forms, that, outside Northumbrian, *seðe* (= *se* or *ðe*) was West-Saxon and late, and that *seðe* forms in *Beowulf* and some prose writings are due to the scribe.

INDEX

Arabic numerals refer to sections